Sustainability and
Globalization

Sustainability and
Globalization

Edited by
Julio de Santa Ana

WCC Publications, Geneva

Cover design: Michael Martin

ISBN: 2-8254-1265-1

© 1998 WCC Publications, World Council of Churches,
150 route de Ferney, 1211 Geneva 2, Switzerland

Printed in Switzerland

Table of Contents

vii Introduction   *Julio de Santa Ana*

1 Is a Sustainable Society Possible in the Context of Globalization?

BIBLE STUDIES

23 Luke 10:25-37   *Petra von Gemunden*

29 Revelation 12   *Petra von Gemunden*

SUSTAINABILITY

35 How Sustainable Is the Present Project of World Trade?
Lukas Vischer

57 Sustainability, Full Employment and Globalization:
Contradictions or Complements?   *Francis Wilson*

65 Defining Terms   *Edward Dommen*

71 Sustainable Development and Biotechnology
Jackie Leach Scully

77 Climate Change and Sustainable Development   *Janos Pasztor*

GLOBALIZATION

89 Discerning the Causes of Globalization   *Daniel Rush Finn*

99 Globalization: Blessing or Curse? Buzz-word or Swear-word?
Peter Tulloch

107 Globalization and Sustainable Prosperity   *Herbert Oberhänsli*

111 Globalization: Some Socio-Cultural Comments
Melba Padilla Maggay

118 The Impact of Globalization on Labour and Workers' Lives
Dominique Peccoud

THEOLOGICAL INSIGHTS

123 Sustainability and Globalization: Demystifying the Single Thought and Single Structure
Joannes Petrou

130 Reclaiming Motherhood: In Search of an Eco-feminist Vision
Aruna Gnanadason

144 About the Contributors

Introduction

Since 1993, the Ecumenical Institute of Bossey has sponsored a series of W.A. Visser 't Hooft consultations, focusing on matters of concern for Christian social ethics. The first, in June 1993, discussed the tension between economic growth and sustainability, asking whether it is possible to affirm "sustainable growth" or whether this very concept is a contradiction in terms. The second, in June 1995, focused on the relations between labour and sustainability, considering the question of employment from the perspective of a sustainable society. The third, in June 1997, considered "Sustainability and Globalization". From different angles – economic, technological, social and cultural – the participants discussed the possibility of sustainable society and sustainable development in the context of the ongoing process of accelerated globalization. The present collection is the outcome of that consultation.

W.A. Visser 't Hooft, general secretary of the World Council of Churches from the time of the decision to form it in 1938 until 1966, envisioned the Ecumenical Institute of Bossey as a place for reflection about and exploration of the ecumenical dimension of the life of the churches. At the creation of the Ecumenical Institute he said that

> it should be a place where men and women from all the member churches of the ecumenical movement can learn together to give and to receive, can learn to struggle for one another, thus accepting the tension between truth and unity which is at the heart of all true ecumenical community. The programme of the Institute thus comprises three main subject areas: the Bible, the world, the universal church.[1]

The series of consultations to honour the memory of the first general secretary of the WCC has tried to maintain the tension between these three elements. This was also the case during the consultation on "Sustainability and Globalization". The contributions to the consultation collected here belong to Visser 't Hooft's "three main subject areas". There are Bible studies which look for the production of meaning in the context of the tensions between the ethical imperative for a sustainable society and the undeniable reality of prevailing globalization. Other essays shed light on such problems and challenges related to sustainability as climate change, biological diversity and sustainable development. There are also reflections which try to understand from different points of view the many-faceted reality of the process of globalization. Finally, this volume includes some inputs which try to understand the tensions between sustainability and globalization from a theological point of view.

On the basis of the findings of the consultation, a group of participants formulated a statement which is offered as a contribution to the ongoing ecumenical debate on these matters. They tried to make clear that while there are different conceptions of "sustainability", a convergence among these different understandings is emerging. Furthermore, they tried to highlight the complex situation around the meaning of "globalization", which is perceived in different ways by different people. Some would limit its meaning to the economic level of life. Others emphasize its social aspects. Still others recognize the cultural dimension of the term, to the point of saying that it has become an important factor in the ideological tensions of our time.

Obviously, the impact of the process of globalization on the environment and on our societies cannot be ignored. Some perceive globalization as the way to move towards the future, while others, especially in developing countries, point to the heavy burden its imperatives put on the lives of poor people. So, they encourage the need to confront this process.

This is a special task of communities concerned with the defence and promotion of life – or, to say it in theological terms, communities which try to be responsible for God's creation. Theological reflection is thus an important contribution in this debate.

We offer this volume to the public in the hope that the essays collected here will contribute to reflection and debate in the churches about this issue, especially at the eighth assembly of the World Council of Churches.

Julio de Santa Ana

NOTE

[1] "L'église chrétienne dans la crise mondiale", *Cahiers de l'Institut oecuménique*, no. 1, 1946, p.4.

Is a Sustainable Society Possible in the Context of Globalization?

The ecumenical movement, like the rest of the world, was surprised by the sudden collapse of "socialist" (communist) countries in the last weeks of 1989, and unprepared for the consequences. Although there had been clear signs as early as 1985 that the "socialist" nations in Eastern Europe (and subsequently China and other "socialist" countries) were abandoning some of their ideological rigidity, the complete disintegration of the Eastern European ideological system was unexpected by churches.

The European Ecumenical Assembly on "Peace with Justice", held in Basel in May 1989, had agreed that, in light of the growing openness in relations between East and West, the task of the European churches was primarily "to facilitate dialogue" between the two rival ideological blocs and thus to encourage peaceful coexistence. Six months later, the major ideological conflict which had divided the world and the ecumenical movement for more than forty years was virtually at an end.

During this same period, the World Council of Churches was making final preparations for the world convocation on Justice, Peace and the Integrity of Creation (JPIC), convened in Seoul in March 1990. That meeting showed how difficult it is for churches today to find consensus on relevant responses to the challenges facing societies in different parts of the world, particularly those related to sustainability.

The significance of this momentous political-economic change was further debated at the WCC assembly in Canberra in February 1991. Assembly Section II was less positive about the outcome of the economic-ideological change which had occurred than the WCC central committee had been in March 1990. The assembly report declares:

> After the economic system of the so-called "socialist" countries plunged into deep crisis, many hopes were expressed about the system of the free-market

economy. But it appeared that the free-market economy is also unable to adjust to the new world economic order without new social and ecological institutions.[1]

Section II also affirmed that "part of our task is the education of people to raise their consciousness about the world economic and political situation in order to provide them with the tools to practise freedom and justice". The WCC was urged to take up this work.

WCC reflection on the challenge of globalization

The ecumenical reflection called for by the Canberra assembly renewed impetus to work earlier undertaken by the WCC's Advisory Group on Economic Matters (AGEM). In August 1991 the WCC central committee recommended that AGEM undertake a study of the economic issues facing the churches in the new "global" context. In August 1992 a report by this group of economists and theologians, *Christian Faith and the World Economy Today*, was approved by the WCC central committee and commended for study in the churches. Widely distributed in the churches, this study document stimulated new reflection on the Christian approach to global economic issues after the cold war, especially regarding the responsibility of the rich nations.

The report acknowledged that the demise of communism made possible a new "global" approach to issues of social-economic order and justice. It spoke of

> interlocking and worldwide realities, which require worldwide processes of handling and solving. It may sound somewhat unreal to speak in these terms when the "normal" contexts of thought and action for most people are the smaller units of family, village, tribe, township or region, and where so much power of decision – and of the educational and ideological shaping of decisions – resides in the nation-states whose common forum in the United Nations system is still far from growing into the forerunner of a world government. Yet one of the unmistakable features of our time is that the trend to greater "globalization" seems irreversible. Environmental threats pay no respect to national borders. Neither do diseases such as AIDS or problems such as drug addiction. Global problems must be seen for what they are, however difficult it is to know how to resolve them.[2]

The report listed nine priority issues for ecumenical reflection:

1. *The shocking extent of "absolute poverty"* and of indifference to it "at a time in world history when the conditions necessary to ensure a minimal living standard for all are entirely (if not straightforwardly) within the powers of the world community".

2. *The growing gap between rich and poor* and "the deterioration in relations between the richer nations of 'the North' and the poorer nations of 'the South'".

3. *The global debt crisis* with many nations "trapped in a permanently crippling vice of financial debt, from which there is no prospect of release anywhere in sight".

4. *Threats to the environment* arising out of "environmentally destructive economic developments... fuelled by social, cultural and ideological processes. Certain theological thinking has not remained immune to this and may even have contributed to it."

5. *Land as an economic commodity*, "treated as an object of speculation and reduced to one more possible source of financial profit".

6. *The differing roles of women and men.* Despite some signs of progress, "those whose views count for most in economic matters still undervalue what women are contributing, let alone what they could if their gifts were more adequately released and rewarded. It is estimated that work of all kinds done by women amounts to more than two-thirds of the hours worked overall, though they receive no more than a tiny fraction of the money income paid... In almost every culture the women are 'naturally' expected to take charge of all that requires doing in the household... Although such work is unpaid, it is nonetheless a crucial ingredient in the economy because it holds together the social fabric of society and forms the base for many activities in the economic realm."

7. *Unemployment and under-employment* in nearly every country. "In India or China, where population has long outstripped available land, under-employment is nothing new, though the weight of it rises... In Western European nations, with their understandably proud record of establishing 'welfare states' after the second world war, the combination of recession and the swing to 'free market' ideological policies in the 1980s is biting hard."

8. *Conflict, war and militarization.* "The dissolution of the Warsaw Pact released one major tension that has had incalculable economic consequences over the last forty years... The hopes for a sizeable economic 'peace dividend' have not yet found much realization... partly no doubt because of the fears of unemployment. The Gulf war and the civil conflicts in the Caucasus and the former Yugoslavia are dismaying signs that new tensions may inspire no less priority to be given to military readiness."

9. The key role and often hidden power of *communication systems*. "Today, new technologies offer possibilities of wider communication

and education for all. At the same time their misuse threatens their true purpose... The economic and political control over media deeply influences what many people are able to think and imagine. The misuse of media can spread consumerism, racism, sexism and religious intolerance."

Already in 1975, the fifth assembly of the WCC noted the "new emphasis" being given to "the goal of a sustainable society, where each individual can feel secure that quality of life will be maintained or improved".[3]

In recent years the notion of sustainability has again been the object of ecumenical reflection and debate. The challenge to affirm sustainability has become more dramatic in the context of the accelerated integration of markets made possible by rapid technological changes, especially in the fields of mobility and communications. Can sustainable societies be achieved within the framework of the present project of world trade? How can the challenges of both justice and sustainability be met under the conditions imposed by the trends of globalization? What orientations in the area of social thought and social action will enable Christians and churches to give a relevant witness to Christian faith in our time?

The three consultations organized by the Visser 't Hooft Foundation and the Ecumenical Institute of Bossey have sought to contribute to a deeper understanding of the implications of the term "sustainability" for Christian social ethics. They have focused on "Sustainable Growth" (1993), "Work in Sustainable Societies" (1995) and "Sustainability and Globalization" (1997).

Sustainability

The term "sustainability" basically refers to the need for human beings to recognize the limits inherent in creation and to adapt their claims on the future to a course which can be sustained – that is, maintained for an indefinite time.

The basic dilemma which has led to the more and more general use of the term was set forth by an ecumenical conference already in 1974:

> For a short period in recent history some societies cultivated the dream of unlimited wealth, of overcoming poverty, not primarily by sharing wealth but by increasing it so that there would be enough for all. Now we face a sobering return to reality. We begin to perceive that the future will require a husbanding of resources and a reduction of expectations of global economic growth. We do not expect that humanity can live as the most extravagant have been living, and we no longer believe that the spillover of wealth from the top will

mean prosperity for all. There may be a divine irony in the fact that the very technological victories which once supported the vision of affluence now – by their contribution to increasing consumption of resources, growing population and pollution – are bringing an end to the dream of a carefree and affluent future.[4]

Through the Brundtland report on environment and development, published in 1987 under the title *Our Common Future*, the term "sustainable development" found wide acceptance. This report spoke of the need for a "development that meets the needs of the present without compromising the ability of future generations to meet their own needs". In the ensuing debate the term has been used in many different ways.

An adequate definition of sustainability must take account of three basic elements:

1. Sustainability implies concern for the well-being of future generations and their right to a fulfilled life. While each generation constructs its own life and alters the face of the earth, no generation should change the quality of the conditions of life on the planet so profoundly as to deprive future generations of major possibilities to build and construct their life and alter the face of the earth in their own right. This means that each generation must take the greatest possible care not to cause irreversible damage. The first Visser 't Hooft consultation in 1993 defined a sustainable society as "one which leaves the world as rich in resources and opportunities as it inherited... This means that renewable resources are consumed no more rapidly than renewable substitutes can be found, that wastes are discharged at a rate no greater than they can be processed by nature or human devices."[5]

As clear as these principles may be, they are bound to lead to conflicts. How are the rights of future generations to be measured against the claims of the present generation? In practice, the rights of future generations generally take second place. On closer examination, therefore, this principle of responsibility for future generations is much more demanding than it may appear at first.

2. The second consideration concerns justice. The Brundtland report speaks of the common future of humankind and rightly emphasizes that "the essential needs of the world's poor need to be given over-riding priority" in all efforts to preserve the "environment's ability to meet present and future needs". For the churches this consideration is of particular importance. They stand for the cause of justice. To struggle on behalf of the world's poor is an essential part of their witness.

If sustainability must not be achieved at the expense of justice, the pressing question is how justice can be achieved within the planet's limited potential. The diversity of moral judgments reveals the need for more careful assessment of this potential. One of the strengths of the Brundtland report is that it speaks of the problems of environment, poverty and energy as a single connected crisis. But even if it is generally accepted that only development which opens up a future to all nations may justly be termed sustainable, the implications of this principle are rarely recognized. The dangers that threaten the human race are assessed from the point of view of one's own future.

Taking seriously the need for a "common future" represents a particular challenge to industrialized nations, which not only consume a disproportionately high share of resources but also contribute by their life-style to the destruction of the ecological equilibrium in the South. The quest for sustainability thus exposes a new form of exploitation of the South by the North. A new degree of sharing is required.

3. The third consideration concerns the assessment of threats and risks. How do we responsibly evaluate the risks humanity is facing today? Answers differ widely. Often scientists offer estimates and scenarios which demonstrate that solutions are fundamentally possible in many areas. But the countless studies which show that the agenda of sustainability can in principle be met assume both the will to put these solutions into practice and the ability to set in motion the required political processes, while tending to disregard the unforeseeable character of historical developments. Environmental studies, for example, normally do not refer to the possibility of war and the need for peaceful resolution of conflicts. Often they also overlook the interconnected and mutually reinforcing character of the various threats to the future.

The quest for sustainability thus raises the issue of responsible risk assessment. Four considerations are important in this regard:

a. The gravity of a risk cannot be judged in isolation. The danger posed by a particular risk grows when a situation is already exposed to other risks.

b. Early action is generally less costly than removing damage once it has occurred. Consequently, when the extent of possible damage cannot be predicted or calculated it is sensible to apply the precautionary principle.

c. For Christian conscience the issue of possible or probable victims is of decisive importance. It is one thing to accept risk for oneself, quite another to run it for others. Most studies on risk assessment overlook

Is a Sustainable Society Possible in the Context of Globalization? 7

this. Economic and environmental risks will hit humanity differently in different parts of the world. In risk assessment the vulnerability of the weakest countries must be given over-riding attention.
d. Measures to avoid risks bring costs and disadvantages. How far should present interests or future harm be taken into consideration? In the debate which followed the publication of the Brundtland report there has been much talk about "no regret measures" – protective action that will be economically useful even if the fear caused by the supposed risk should prove to be unfounded. Often the term is used to delay decisions called for by a sober assessment of a risk. Basically, only measures which ensure long-term sustainability will cause no regret.

Can sustainability be achieved within the framework of the present economic system? By combining the terms "sustainable" and "development" the Brundtland report seems to assume an affirmative answer. But this cannot be taken for granted. Deeper changes may be required than simple corrections of present trends. The Brundtland report rightly points to the possibility of further technological achievements and expresses the conviction that the exploitation of resources can in principle be drastically reduced by a more efficient social organization. There is no doubt that new perspectives may arise within the present framework. But the question remains whether such modifications will be able to meet the requirements for a sustainable society or whether more fundamental changes in the orientation of society are called for. With this question in mind the consultation has sought to assess the present trend towards a new model of organizing world trade into one global market.

Globalization

Although we are living in a period of transition and the ongoing historical situation is far from being crystallized, it is now possible to say that economic globalization is a process which combines several elements. In the first place, it is the contemporary expression of a strong historical trend which created the world economic system through the internationalization of some markets and the transnationalization of economic enterprises. Second, the globalization of markets has been accelerated in recent decades by technological developments, especially in the realm of computer science and communications. Third, a global market, more integrated than ever before, has been shaped for raw materials, manufactured goods, financial and derivative products. As a result, prevailing global trends are expressions of the different ways the market functions. They are based on the accumulation of instruments, especially at the technological level, which have enabled the creation and development of complex economic devices (for example, the world economic system, different markets at the international level and economic tools aiming at the management of both the system and markets). The combination of these elements results in the acceleration of different types of exchanges, creating new burdens for human beings and making it difficult for them to respond to this constant pressure of urgency.

Many world leaders have unambiguously endorsed globalization, arguing that it is the key to global prosperity. Behind this promise of an improvement of economic life lies an implicit hope: that the process of increasing daily productivity of ordinary working people, which has undergirded relative prosperity for the large majority of citizens in the industrialized world, will do the same for all the people of the earth, substantially improving the current global distribution of income and wealth. Firms of all sizes contribute to the gains of both consumers and the labour force, provided they are competitive. In the process of globalization, hundreds of millions of new jobs are being created, though in new sectors and areas, since industries change under competitive pressure (usually the more labour-intensive industries moving out of higher industrialized economies; in developing countries it is the formerly protected industries which suffer most). In addition, the end of the USSR and changes in Eastern Europe have led many to argue that "there is no alternative" to the market system.

But other voices would resoundingly reject this single frame of reference *(la pensée unique)* as an ideological defence of the great and growing privilege of the wealthy, who benefit so richly from the globalization of life. The promise of globalization is experienced by many in our world as an empty one. Thus it is said that a process which so thoroughly threatens humanity, culture and environment must be rejected.

From the ecumenical perspective, it is clear that the way forward must involve dialogue among different positions and currents of thought, accepting pluralism and the need for constructive cooperation which aims to define actions based on consensus whenever possible.

This diversity of moral judgments reveals the need for more careful assessment of the different dimensions of what is referred to as "globalization". It is evident that the term covers a number of independent but inter-related activities which have been "globalized": finance, communications, trade, power, technology and an ideological conception of the world. Furthermore there is a globalization of problems in health and the natural environment, exemplified by the HIV/AIDS pandemic and the spread of plant and animal life-forms to regions of the world where they upset an historic ecological balance. Cultural exchanges, which enable peoples to share their values and traditions but also create new tensions, are also described in terms of globalization.

Overarching typologies such as this are always problematic. In seeking to clarify our use of the term "globalization", we should be mindful of several factors. First, technology needs to be recognized as not just one of the things that have become "globalized" but as the underlying factor making a globalized world possible and to a large extent defining its character. In fact, the apparent inevitability of much of this ongoing process of technological change further complicates our moral assessment. The process is with us; we cannot return to an earlier era. Christians must evaluate each possibility and discern those developments which favour and those which threaten our fundamental commitment to sustain humanity, culture and the environment.

Second, there are many who accept the prevailing economic system on the basis of empirical considerations while others reject this single frame of reference. There are indeed some positive outcomes of the prevailing process. The technological changes which make possible the integration of markets also contribute to a more human life for many women and men. Unfortunately, there are also destructive elements in this process.

Indeed, to address issues of "globalization" adequately, we should speak in particular terms of international trade or investment or the transfer of technology. Even better, we should speak concretely, for example, of trade in a particular commodity by given firms in various nations, each with its own unique distribution of land ownership, income, wealth and political power. It is only at this level of detail that the defensible and indefensible aspects of the globalization process can be discerned.

Throughout our assessment we are called to use an operational criterion which enables us at least to begin to assess whether a given action or policy sustains humanity, namely, whether it benefits "the least of these who are members of my family" (Matt. 25:40). When any aspect of globalization fails this critical test, a point of resistance has been identified.

Tensions between sustainability and globalization

There are several areas in which elements of the process of globalization affect the requirements of sustainability. Without claiming to provide an exhaustive list, we may mention the following:

1. *Ethical tension.* Globalization implies an economically rational behaviour which is rooted in the philosophical tradition of utilitarianism. For many persons, sustainability is an ethical imperative; and they would advance a social and ecological ethic which takes into account not only economic imperatives, but also justice, social responsibility and participation.

2. *Unlimited growth, reasonable human satisfaction and unfair distribution of resources.* Because the world has limited resources, the prevailing economic trend which aims at permanent economic growth – which characterizes the process of globalization – threatens the sustainability of life and future generations. Furthermore, the product of economic growth is unevenly shared, and the gap between the well-off and the poor is widening. Those who aim at sustainability affirm that the rich minority of the world, which profits from the process of globalization, is wasting a great volume of earth's resources and living far above the level of human need. The debate between those who want more economic growth and those who advocate an "economy of enough" is becoming sharper.

3. *Technology and sustaining humanity.* Technology, which can contribute much to the improvement of life, especially when its innovations take account of the vital needs of human beings and the natural and social environment, is also used to destroy jobs and weaken human communities. This particularly applies to the tensions generated by the exploitation of resources of the South by economic powers who have the knowledge and control of these technologies. Furthermore, a technology which may promote life for some (at least according to prevailing, mostly Western patterns of thought) can at the same time be negative for many others. For example, without any consultation with the wider public, powerful economic agents make critical decisions about genetic manipulations that may threaten human life.

4. *Communications and sustaining humanity.* While developments in modern technologies of information broaden people's possibilities for communicating and inter-relating, there is a very strong trend towards the concentration of global information on trade in the hands of a few powerful commercial actors, whose goals are not made clear to the majority of the public. Yet it should be recognized that people's associations, non-governmental organizations and churches are beginning to use the new computer resources to generate and share information that will enable the poor and marginalized to address some of their problems.

5. *Acceleration of the rhythm of human relationships and transactions.* The technological developments on which the process of eco-

Is a Sustainable Society Possible in the Context of Globalization?

nomic globalization is based enable quicker contact among people than ever before in history. The acceleration of trade requires financial transactions and information about markets which contribute greatly to economic growth. Computer programmes are designed to react almost instantaneously to fluctuations in the market. Trade can also facilitate easier contact among people. But this new phenomenon inherent to the process of globalization also creates a level of stress and anxiety which is difficult to manage; and some are asking whether this situation is human or sustainable.

6. *The influence of production trends and finance.* The necessary inter-relation of places of production in today's world helps to make visible the basic solidarity of human beings. One of the disturbing realities of our time, however, is the dominating power of financial capital. The specific interests of global finance seem to impose their power on nearly every aspect of human life. Although the majority of investments in many financial markets may come from pension funds for employees, civil servants, churches and the like, their managers often behave aggressively; and in the final analysis those most affected are the impoverished, who find little space in which to exercise human freedom or to seek alternatives to sustain their lives.

7. *Trade and foreign direct investment.* Increased international trade and direct foreign investment hold out the hope that the people of the developing world may participate in the prosperity enjoyed by others. After generations of almost exclusively providing primary products to the industrialized world, the building of factories in developing countries to process those products for export and to manufacture a large variety of goods for both export and domestic consumption has enabled some people to move out of poverty. Others however have become poorer and experience a growing feeling of insecurity; and the fact is that most developing countries are not enjoying these potential benefits of trade and direct foreign investment.

Moreover, the terms of trade regularly worsen for most underprivileged peoples while they improve for some of the wealthy. This significantly reduces any advantages of trade for those most in need while increasing the advantage of those who already have greater advantage. Transnational corporations press governments – especially, though not only, in the developing world – for concessions on taxes, labour regulations and environmental standards by threatening to move elsewhere if they are not granted. Social justice is thus undermined, and governments are deprived of the revenue to maintain necessary public services. Similarly, international competition leads firms to press governments to delay implementing stricter controls to combat climate change and local pollution. Both physical and social sustainability are thus threatened.

8. *Economic globalization and social exclusion.* As a result of market integration millions of jobs are lost at the level of production, meaning that more and more people are affected by chronic unemployment, lack the necessary means for a decent life and confront the painful realization that their socio-economic rights are of little or no importance. The mergers and take-overs which are a chief index of globalization are often followed by an announcement that jobs are being cut. At the level of international trade, certain regions of the world, such as Africa and Central America, have a smaller share today than twenty years ago. This greatly affects the life of many people, whose only chance for survival is the informal sector, "the underground economy", where their social rights are not respected.

9. *Motorized mobility and increasing migration.* Mobility has always been a driving force of trade; and the present level of world trade would not be possible without the development of more and faster transportation of both persons and goods. Further expanding world trade favours the further increase of motorized mobility. From the point of view of sustainability, this must be avoided. Those concerned with the environmental crisis believe that new approaches to mobility and transport must be found.

A further element of mobility is reflected in the increasing numbers of uprooted people. The phenomenon of economic refugees has reached an intensity unforeseen as recently as ten years ago. When the conditions to survive decently are lacking in their native places, people decide to migrate – from rural areas to the cities, from small towns to the big urban centres, from poor countries to wealthier ones. However, prevailing economic trends are unable to create the conditions necessary to enable societies to face this situation adequately. Indeed, the integration of markets is managed in a way that works against this. The result is a growth of lawlessness and violence both in the North and the South. Current demographic trends, especially in some regions of the South, tend to aggravate this.

10. *Intercultural tensions.* When economic globalization is affirmed as the only route to a better human future, those cultures which experience its impact as a threat or even an attack will inevitably clash with prevailing trends. Cultural fragmentation is almost inescapable. People's lives are torn. They cannot reject integration into international markets

and the accompanying imperatives to be more efficient and competitive; at the same time, they sense that their traditions, values and identities (which often include a respectful and caring attitude to the natural environment) are in danger. These tensions are sometimes unfortunately manifested in violent terms.

11. *The role of the state.* A key structural consequence of globalization has been a weakening of political control over economic life. In an earlier era, the shift of power from the local to the national level, which was a characteristic element in the formation of the modern nation-state, disrupted local community but provided the ground for a less parochial assessment of the social conditions necessary for human life. But the contemporary reduction of national political power and sovereignty has not been compensated for by the creation of a transnational political authority which could appropriately and democratically define the limits within which market activity must occur. International economic and especially financial exchanges strive to limit the control of national authorities.

In this context, the regulatory role of the state in the economic realm must be underlined. If the state should not be an economic actor among others, competing with them, it ought nevertheless to set the framework and to be responsible for the economic process at the national level, including its economic exchanges with other nations. Both Christian ethics and good secular policy analysis require a careful coordination of these processes. It is irresponsible for the wealthiest groups of the world to press for quick international agreements that so evidently serve their own interests while postponing and resisting morally necessary agreements in areas such as labour standards and environmental policies because they would place limits on the freedom of firms and the consumption of the prosperous. It is the responsibility of the state to guarantee that the common national interest is respected; and to do so it must fulfil its regulatory role.

Communities in a context of globalization

Human beings seek meaning and the experience of belonging to associations with other persons with whom they can develop face-to-face and not only "virtual" relationships. Such contacts are far easier in places where tradition prevails and people know each other on a personal level than in societies more strongly affected by modernity.

It is important to recognize the role that different types of human communities play. Though not all persons participate in community life, those who do participate experience a strengthening of their personal identity. This kind of human relationship is more meaningful than that which characterizes life in mass society. In community life people share common concerns, mutual support and solidarity. To be sure, human communities are never perfect, but they do create a space where dialogue is possible and where life can be more human.

Some communities share interests which enable their members to involve themselves in some common action. Through this they express common convictions and common responsibilities. The community then becomes something more than a mere human association. It is like an organism, which expresses itself as a collective being in particular tones about matters which are of common concern. Thus communities can be clearly distinguished within mass society. Though their members may be involved in all kinds of social processes, they are particularly known by how they relate to other members of their community and by the kind of common thought and action that they develop.

All human societies, in one way or another, are influenced by the different elements involved in the process of globalization. The impact of new technologies of communications and the integration of markets have a direct or indirect impact on people's lives. The social relationships which globalization favours are those which are "virtual" and less personal. That is, the prevailing trends of the global economy privilege that which is more characteristic of the life of mass society – mass communications, mass consumption, homogenization of patterns of life, mass culture. (Again, however, we must be reminded that globalization is a complex process, and both comprehensive endorsement or blanket rejection of it is morally and conceptually simplistic.)

In the context of mass society, human beings run the risk of being depersonalized. A tension emerges between society and communities, especially those communities which support causes and concerns that are not well respected in social life, whether in the economic, political, cultural or even religious realm. This happens, for example, to communities which affirm and defend the sustainability of nature and of human societies. At the level of the village or the nation or the region or the planet, they try to initiate social processes which can make life more human, more personal. To put it another way, they try to introduce a dose of what they believe is *good sense* in the *common sense* which prevails among the majority of the people.

These communities cannot avoid tension and confrontation with prevailing trends of economic globalization. And if they are not aware of their vulnerability and limitations, they risk losing their identity. But at the same time, they can strengthen themselves if they are also aware of their *charisma*, of the authority that they can exert in society so long as they are faithful to their vocation. If power in mass society is linked to numbers of people, the authority of communities can be based only on their quality. They can make an impact, even if their action is not comparable with the magnitude of the powers which give direction to life in mass society. This impact depends on the inherent character of the community, its courage to be and to support its convictions. It is a matter of ethical decision.

Present global trends and community life
Some elements of the process of globalization as we have described it open up possibilities for community life. Technological developments accelerate and multiply at least virtual communications. Information is disseminated more widely; international networks are built up. Accompanying these opportunities is the emergence of an international civil society as the expression of the will of many civil (non-governmental) people's associations, which affirm public interests such as respect for the environment, justice for the needy and human rights. In some way or another, people's movements also benefit from some facets of globalization.

However, globalization also threatens community life. First, given its dependence on the world of human constructions and the extraordinary nature of most of the elements which make it possible, globalization accentuates the instrumental intention of economic activities. It reinforces a "culture of enterprise" which reduces most created beings to things and means. Human beings, who can understand themselves only by taking account of their living relationships with their environment, run the risk of having an important part of themselves amputated. The breaking of communion between nature and human beings tempts persons to ignore not only their links with their environment but also their own limits. The sacramental dimension of life, its mystery, is no longer recognized.

Unfortunately, experiences show that instrumentality seldom takes account of the unintended consequences of instrumental action. One of these is precisely its effect on the character of human communities. Reduced to tools in social processes, they risk losing their potential to be spaces in which human beings can create meaning for their lives.

A second threat comes from the peculiar ideological proposal – *la pensée unique* – which accompanies the process of globalization and aspires to be the only valid one, imposing itself as the paradigm to which all other cultures should be adjusted. Human communities come to be and live in their own specific cultural contexts. The difference among these contexts should be respected. The homogenization of human behaviour which global markets implicitly intend to impose endangers community life by threatening people's relationships with their own cultures and by depersonalizing human relationships.

Third, when many human beings use mostly virtual communications to relate to each other, adopting a dominant code of signs as common language, and therefore neglecting other languages, the result is a loss in the quality of being of a community. Virtual relationships depersonalize human contacts. Mass culture, conveyed by an increasing use of mass media, continues to expand. It also results in mass consumption. The danger of cultural fragmentation is almost unavoidable.

Fourth, the particularly devastating effects of the prevailing trends of the globalizing economy on the community life of indigenous peoples must be particularly emphasized. Exploitation of natural resources and lack of care for land often threaten the very being of these communities.

Communities and caring for life

Those who want to manage the processes and integration of markets favour globalization. They look on its development optimistically, encouraged by the unprecedented growth in world trade. They believe the integration of markets will bring along with it the integration of cultures and peoples.

However, many others are fearful and anxious about the high price they must pay to adjust themselves to globalization. Still others simply feel lost. Those who are excluded from the process of globalization experience pain, suffering and meaninglessness. They feel that they are not recognized but are considered as objects, as masses, but not as human beings with rights and responsibilities. As part of the mass of excluded people – whether they live in industrialized, developing or less developed nations – they sense that they are despised and discarded, as if they do not count at all. They do not have the chance to live well, but only to survive. The underground economy seems to be their only chance.

Amidst this paradoxical coexistence of the integration of markets and the exclusion of people are some communities in which men and women associate to affirm life. Not surprisingly, many of the individuals who participate in groups defending human rights are also involved in the ecological movement and in other movements acting for social renewal.

The common thread is their affirmation of life – an expression of their awareness that we share a common existence in a world where injustice prevails and life is in danger. These communities ask whether sustainability has a chance within the context of ongoing globalization. Can a sustainable society emerge in the framework of prevailing trends of growing world trade and human mobility? Is it possible to launch processes of "sustainable development"?

Such communities are ready to resist the threats globalization poses to human beings and to sustain and affirm a kind of life which is common to all and can be shared with future generations. These communities, which care for life and intend to resist irresponsible behaviour, are aware not only of their limited possibilities but also of their convictions and of their responsibilities.

These are *ethical communities*. They practise ethical discernment, on the basis of which they perceive both what must be affirmed and what is unacceptable. In order to affirm their convictions they undertake actions for sustainability. Confronted with what should not be accepted, they involve themselves in resistance. Both – affirmation and resistance – are two sides of the same coin: *caring for life*. These communities show themselves to be aware that the fundamental solidarity among all human beings, and above all with the poor and oppressed, cannot and should not be dissolved, that the mystery of the communion between human beings and the natural environment must be acknowledged and respected, that life is more than *my* life and so I cannot treat life as an object.

Ethical communities, aware of their convictions and responsibilities, have values for which they are ready to pay the price. Values remain in the realm of the subjective up to the moment when those who affirm them are prepared to substantiate that affirmation with a costly action. Sometimes this means resisting ideas and social behaviours which are shared by the majority of the people, resisting the prevailing *common sense*, because it is not *good sense*. The uncritical affirmation and absolutization of the globalization process is not *good sense*, no matter how large the masses who see it as the only way into the future. Rather than accepting and supporting an instrumental approach to reality, *good sense* expresses the conviction that the mystery (sacrament) of life is to be cared for, and that responsible action must follow this awareness.

Christian churches as communities of meaning and grace

Many Christians are involved in different types of communities which are concerned for the sustainability of life. There are Christian communities that witness to their faith by striving for justice and solidarity and caring for the environment. These communities try to understand the situations in which they live and to analyze their different aspects. They also study the Bible for inspiration and guidance for action. And when they decide to get involved in praxis, they do it collectively, as a fellowship. As they share the means of grace, they also share their commitment.

This awareness of faith overcomes the separation between culture and nature, between history and creation. The love commandment involves God and the human neighbour (individuals, social groups, future generations), but also the rest of creation. Because the mystery of God's grace has no limits, Christian communities witness to this grace and seek to introduce the awareness of this faith into a world whose powers do not want to recognize it.

Christian communities face the challenge of translating their awareness of faith to society, of making more clear the meaning of grace through social structures and institutions. They know that their witness is often only a very limited and symbolic testimony to the presence of grace in what seems a graceless world. Thus they try to be the "salt of the earth" and "the light of the world". A praxis of sustainability and action aimed at shaping a sustainable society, caring for justice, the environment and solidarity, are necessary components of Christian witness in our time.

When globalization is affirmed as the only way, it becomes sacralized. An idol is shaped, a fetish is crafted. A false god justifies the striving for domination of powerful agents who respect neither nature nor their neighbours' rights. Christians are called to confess that God is gracious and just, and that God cannot be confused with Mammon.

Theological insights

The double challenge of sustainability and justice

One of the convictions of faith that provides meaning for Christians is an awareness of the sacramental dimension of all creation. The creation speaks about the Creator (Pss. 19:1-6; 104:1-30). This is not "natural revelation", but an awareness that in mysterious ways the imprint of God and his eternal love and plan are present in creation. Creation is not finished, and Christian communities expect and hope for the fulfilment of God's work, in which they have been graciously invited to collaborate (cf. 2 Cor. 5:16-6:2).

For Christian communities, care for the creation is thus unavoidable. This demands a concerted action of caring for one's neighbour and caring for the social and the natural environment.

Christian faithfulness requires living in a right relationship with the whole of the created world. This means living within the natural limits of the created world, treating it as an integral part of God's creation, and tending to nature in order to increase and to use its bounty without destroying it, so that it may provide for successive generations.

Christian faithfulness also requires living in a right relationship with the rest of humanity, which is also a part of creation. This means recognizing one's obligation to treat the other as an integral part of God's creation, to care for the other as an end in himself or herself, not a mere means to an end. Thus Christians regard both the natural world and the human social world which it shelters as having intrinsic worth and as being intricately connected. They are worthy and of value in and of themselves, as part of creation, just because they are.

Christians remember that Jesus made love of the neighbour one of the core ethical injunctions of the Christian faith. As we consider the processes of globalization, we must admit that these economic processes not only exploit and ruin nature, far exceeding its natural limits and regenerative abilities, but also exploit human beings, condemning many millions of urban and rural workers to generations of poverty, and altogether excluding many millions more from formal economic and political life. Such exploitation and exclusionism is wrong. It is a clear violation of the intrinsic worth of both the human person and the natural world. As Christians we must insist on and work for acceptable alternatives. Not to do so is tantamount to the literal sacrifice of perhaps billions of human beings in successive generations on the altar of market processes and market ideology, human expediency and greed.

The temptation of idolatry

The complacency of the comfortable can easily become a form of idolatry. Without thinking about it, they passively allow the market to assume the properties and dimensions of God in their imaginations and in their behaviour. People come to accept the fate meted out by the market as if submission were the only option. Thus what is in actuality a mere mechanism devised by human beings to foster efficient production and consumption takes on the proportions of an autonomous force governing the lives of individuals and communities.

Again and again the Bible warns against this tendency to create institutions and practices which come over time to be seen as autonomous and independent of their creators, this inclination to submit to their logic, accept them as inevitable and thus worship limited human creations instead of the creator God. Consider, for example, the Golden Calf in Exodus 32, shaped out of the melted gold of many people and then worshipped as God. The biblical name for this behaviour is idolatry, and it is understood as a primary source of human sin.

The biblical writers insisted that we cannot worship God while worshipping our own human creations as if they were God. We cannot serve our neighbour when sacrificing him or her to the false gods we have created and upon which we in our insecurity have come to depend.

The biblical texts remind us that we are not the first to create and to worship false gods. But the magnitude and scope of the processes of the global market seem to make it clear that in no previous idolatry has so much been at stake, both in terms of the survival of many millions of human beings and in terms of the planet earth itself.

One cannot expect to dismantle this idolatry of the global market economy without unmasking this idol, making clear the relationships, bringing to visibility much of what is today hidden and mysterious. Christians must confess and denounce these relationships and then begin the process of reconstruction. Rich and poor, in North and South, must confess their idolatrous relationship with the global market economy in different ways. Some will have to confess to participating in the construction of that economy, others to perpetuating its ideology. Some will have to confess the easy compliance of the comfortable, others their willingness to sacrifice all values and traditions to the illusory promise of the market's glitter.

Too many Christians, especially the rich, have identified Christianity with market economics, attributing to the market Christian virtues and values, and importing market values and practices into their understanding of the Christian faith. In some quarters a critique of the global market is perceived as an attack on Christianity itself. Many have identified material success with spiritual well-being, implicitly and sometimes explicitly concluding that poverty is the proof of the material and spiritual failure of the poor. But the poor know better than the rich that material wealth is no sign of spiritual wealth. From the depths of their own experience they understand Jesus' repeated warning that wealth is more often than not a hindrance rather than a help to faithful clarity of vision and purpose.

The Christian God is not the global market, nor does God require the sacrifice of humans and nature to market processes. Faithfulness today requires not total submission to the lure and the power of global market processes, but rather participation in the creation and re-creation of human institutions and practices which support values of inclusion rather than exclusion, protection rather than destruction, stewardship rather than greed, solidarity rather than the survival of the fittest.

A plea for critical realism

Just as Christians must not succumb to the temptation of idolatry, so they should not be misled by romantic and idealistic visions of a perfect state of things. There is no perfect society. Though obliged to unmask and resist the idolatry inherent in the present system, Christians should not suppose or suggest that there will ever be a society guaranteeing justice, peace and full harmony with creation. Guided by the values of the gospel message, they will seek to participate in setting up structures that promote the widest possible participation. They will seek to strengthen respect for the dignity of all, especially the vulnerable and weak. They will give priority to the demands of solidarity. But they are conscious that human life is replete with competing forces and that the order and functioning of society are inevitably based on compromises. Within the complex network of modern society, the best possible solutions must be responsibly pursued.

The institutions and initiatives which sustain the values of justice, peace and respect for the environment will be multiple and varied. Christians will regard them as limited human instruments, the product of human communities all over the globe, the result of life lived together, thus containing conflicting understandings and interests and established in a form that will change over time. Making room for such institutions requires social, political and economic analysis; and initiatives for evaluation can be thwarted by the absence of a critical overall assessment of the state of society. But the primary concern will be with building up communities that witness to the love of both the neighbour and the whole created world. Some of these communities may not be explicitly Christian. But Christians will not hesitate to work with any group or movement responding to the twofold call to sustainability and justice.

NOTES

[1] Michael Kinnamon, ed., *Signs of the Spirit*, report of the WCC's seventh assembly, Geneva, WCC, 1991, p.78; cf. the "Statement on Issues Arising out of Developments in Central and Eastern Europe", *Minutes of the 41st Meeting of the WCC Central Committee, March 1990*, Geneva, WCC, 1990, pp.50-53.
[2] *Christian Faith and the World Economy Today*, Geneva, WCC, 1992, p.17.
[3] David M. Paton, ed., *Breaking Barriers: Nairobi 1975*, Geneva, WCC, 1976, p.127.
[4] *Study Encounter,* 69, vol. 10, no.4, 1974, p.2.
[5] *Sustainable Growth: A Contradiction in Terms*, Geneva, Visser 't Hooft Endowment Fund for Ecumenical Leadership, 1993, p.5.

Luke 10:25-37

PETRA VON GEMUNDEN

The choice of the question "Who is my neighbour?" as a theme for biblical reflection in a discussion of "sustainability and globalization" may seem ideal, but it also raises two problems which should be noted at the outset.

1. This question – and the passage in the New Testament from which it is drawn – concerns much more the issue of human relations than the ecological dimension of "sustainability", which is not directly mentioned in the text. To put it in theological categories, the question of creation – which is in itself theologically valid – is not immediately raised by the parable of the Good Samaritan.

2. The generally accepted understanding of sustainable development stresses the importance of giving absolute priority to the needs of the poorest of the world. This definition begins from existing inequalities and reflects about the relations between human beings who have the possibility of action and those who have little or no possibility of action. Luke's gospel, however, does not think in categories of structures – even less of "global" structures – but in individual categories. Although the persons in the parable represent "types" pointing beyond the particular individual, the "solution" to the mischief which befalls the man in the parable of the Good Samaritan includes no reflection on why the road between Jerusalem and Jericho was so dangerous (nothing about the relationship between the presence of brigands and the economic instability of the time) or on how this situation might have been remedied (for example by a stronger presence of police or soldiers on the road or programmes of work and reintegration for people trying to survive by robbery).

It is not that such an approach to this problem was unknown in antiquity: Josephus reports that Herod purified Galilee of brigands and as Caesar's representative put an end to the actions of the wrongdoers in

Trachonitis.[1] Agrippa glorified himself for having defeated the brigands;[2] and the impressive extension of the temple under Herod was a major work programme. Later a proposal was made to Agrippa II to rebuild the gallery of the temple to deal with threatening unemployment; he rejected this proposal but did permit the paving of the roads.[3]

The parable of the Good Samaritan is not situated at the level of such "sociological" or structural reflection but rather at the individual level. This could be explained by the fact that the Jesus movement and the earliest Christians were only insignificant minorities without power and real influence in society.

This reasoning on a rather individual level does allow us first to reflect more precisely about all the aspects of the situation to be grasped without being paralyzed by the complexity of the facts. But this starting point does require us to go on and ask whether conclusions can be drawn and applied to more complex situations and problems and, if so, under which conditions.

Despite these reservations, I believe that it is justifiable to start from the rather individual reflection of Luke's gospel, not only because the New Testament represents the fundamental document of our Christian faith but also because the source of any motivation to act on behalf of others lies in the individual – in the human being and not in structures. In discussing all the complex problems of "sustainability" and "globalization", we should not lose sight of the human being and the other. This is the red thread: the neighbour. The biblical tradition formulates it more precisely: "*my* neighbour". This implies that I cannot reflect about the question of the neighbour by analyzing from outside, by excluding myself. In the question of the neighbour I am always directly concerned.

* * *

Luke 10:25-37 is subdivided into two parts: the question of the greatest commandment and the story/example of the Good Samaritan.[4] These two parts shed a light on the question of the neighbour from two different angles: the first part begins from a symmetrical relation, the second from a relation of dependence. The first is situated clearly in the framework of religious thinking whereas the second part seems rather secular. It is not by chance that these two parts form a unity in Luke's gospel: they are related to each other by the idea of "doing". In the first part, the lawyer raises the question: "What must I *do* to inherit eternal life?" And the story/example ends with: "Go and *do* likewise." In both cases the emphasis on "doing" is very clear.

Luke 10:25-28

In this first part Jesus answers the lawyer's question: "Teacher, what must I do to inherit eternal life?" by a counter-question: "What is written in the law? How do you read it?" And the lawyer answers with the double commandment of love: to love God and to love your neighbour. Note that in Luke's account Jesus does not himself give the answer (in contrast to the similar accounts in Matthew 22 and Mark 12) but by referring to the Torah and by asking for his interpretation of it he encourages the lawyer to find and formulate the answer to his own question. Thus Jesus encourages the one who asks him a question to elaborate an independent interpretation (the hermeneutical task). This is a really maieutic approach. According to Luke the central affirmation here does not come from Jesus but from a Jew (who is not necessarily the person with whom the reader of Luke would identify).

What is striking about this double commandment is that the command to love God is clearly distinguished from the command to love the neighbour. For God what is asked for is a love "with all your heart, and with all your soul, and with all your strength, and with all your mind" (v. 27; cf. Deut. 6:5) – that is, a love that involves one's entire existence. The commandment to love the neighbour is much briefer: "Love your neighbour as yourself!"[5] Thus a fundamental distinction is made between the love of God and of the neighbour. The latter is a symmetrical love in which you and others stand at the same level. It is a love in a relationship of reciprocity, of equality. The neighbour of whom the Decalogue speaks is not a poor, dependent, deprived person, but the one who has a house, a wife, slaves, an ox and a donkey which I should not covet (Ex. 20:17) – somebody who is equal to me.

The New Testament maintains this Old Testament idea of the equality of the neighbour even when the status of the persons concerned is not necessarily the same (cf. Rom. 13:18; 15:2). The letter of James links the idea of equality to the idea of the love of the neighbour: "You do well if you really fulfil the royal law according to Scripture, 'You shall love your neighbour as yourself'. But if you show partiality [that is, if you distinguish according to status], you commit sin and are convicted by the law as transgressors" (James 2:8). The idea of equality – that the neighbour stands at the same level as myself – is closely linked to the idea of the love of the neighbour. This idea is inseparable from "doing", as Jesus tells the lawyer: "Do this and you will live." But the lawyer asks for clarification. "And who is my neighbour?" To this Jesus does not respond with a definition (as the lawyer may have hoped), but by a parable, more precisely by a story/example.

Luke 10:29-37

By answering with a story rather than by a precise definition, Jesus appeals not only to our intellect but also to our emotions. His response appeals at the same time to the intellectual, affective and pragmatic dimensions of the human being. By presenting different roles, the story also offers different ways of interpreting the situation and reacting to it. The distance one takes when listening to a fictional story allows a reflection which is much freer, facilitating a restructuration of the perception of reality without triggering immediate resistance. Jesus does not give a definition which one can simply accept or reject. He tells a story which can be approached in several ways: in the priest and the Levite one can perceive aspects of oneself, in the victim of the robbers one can feel the reality of powerlessness, in the Good Samaritan one can find a model.

A deeper understanding of the question of the neighbour requires us to go beyond intellectual and legal definitions through a multiple approach which includes all the dimensions of our existence. The story allows the listener a distance, yet at the same time implies that the listener does not remain a neutral and "untouched" observer analyzing from outside but becomes part of the story. The question of the neighbour does not find an external answer in which one is not directly concerned.

In contrast to the first part of the passage, in which the love of the neighbour is presented as a symmetrical love, this part seems to begin from a relationship marked by a strong inequality: the love of the neighbour is illustrated by someone who is much stronger and descends to the level of the one who is much weaker. This shift is also expressed by a change in vocabulary: one speaks no longer of love but of "pity" (v.33) and "mercy" (v.37). Here is a concept which has evolved in history: the pity granted from the top to the bottom, the mercy and generosity vis-à-vis the most deprived, which in a secular form has characterized a major part of Western societies. This mercy is a behaviour in which the aristocracy and the higher social classes demonstrate their generosity – and indirectly their status. It manifests itself by the sometimes very generous gifts from the North to the South – which stresses the superiority of the societies of the North (and the more or less conscious expectation of a return in the form of gratitude and the easing of a bad conscience). This notion of mercy has become suspicious because it implies inequality and dependence and risks disregarding the sovereignty and the independence of the other person.

When we look more closely at the story-example of the Good Samaritan, we note first of all that the Samaritan did not look for an object of mercy that would allow him to express his generosity and his status. Without seeking it, he encountered a victim.

Second, in contrast to the priest and the Levite, who belonged to the superior social class of the time,[6] the Samaritan was an "outsider" – someone who was not recognized by the Jews. Thus his social status was inferior to that of the victim. This inversion may not be insignificant: the one who is initially considered an outsider helps the one who has suddenly become an outsider, deprived even of his clothes.

Third, the Samaritan does everything which is needed for the victim but not more: he takes care of him, brings him to an inn, feeds him, pays the innkeeper and then leaves the victim. He does not spend the rest of his life looking after this man but takes measures which permit him to lead a normal life again. He does not establish links of permanent aid which would create dependence or aim at gratitude in the future.

Fourth, and I think most striking, is how Jesus ends this story-example. Instead of concluding: "You see, this is your neighbour," he asks, "Which of these three do you think has become a neighbour to the man who fell into the hands of robbers?" Jesus does not summarize his story-example by a definition but concludes with a question which again encourages the lawyer to reflect and to respond. In addition, Jesus turns the lawyer's original question around: "Who is my neighbour?" becomes "Who was a neighbour to the man who fell into the hands of robbers?" Jesus does not answer the question of the neighbour by pointing to an object but by speaking of a subject: the neighbour is the one who approaches the one who becomes a neighbour for the other.

Thus the question of the neighbour is not a question of defining someone who is more or less close and would be the neighbour because of status, ethnic group or religion. Rather it is a question of the one who becomes a neighbour for the other through his action. The question is defined by the "doing". This is why Jesus said, "Go and do likewise." This reversal of the perspective from the object to the subject reminds us of the ideal of the equal, symmetrical love of the first part of the passage.

* * *

The first and second parts of our passage form a unity in Luke's text: the highly religious argument referring to the Torah is juxtaposed with a story that appeals to human experiences which are accessible and understandable independent of religious options.

Next to the love of the neighbour which starts from a symmetrical notion, the equality of the neighbour, we find a relationship of inequality and profound asymmetry which in turn is finally reversed to make out of the object of the "neighbour" the subject of the "neighbour".

NOTES

[1] Cf. Josephus, *Antiquities*, XVI, 9, 158-60; XV, 10, 1, 345-48.
[2] Cf. *Orientis Graeci Inscriptiones Selectae*, 1903-1905, p.424. According to Strabo, Pompey defeated sovereigns and brigands; in this context he mentions the region of Jericho, but doubts whether they were really bandits; they may have been rebels from a military garrison to protect travellers on the road from Jerusalem to Jericho; cf. *Geography*, 16,2,37-40. See also Th. Zahn, *Das Evangelium des Lucas: Kommentar zum Neuen Testament*, Leipzig and Erlangen, Deichert, 1920, p.432, n.11.
[3] See G. Theissen, "Jesus' Temple Prophecy", in *Social Reality and the Early Christians: Theology, Ethics and the World of the New Testament*, tr. M. Kohl, Edinburgh, T. & T. Clark, 1993, pp.94-114.
[4] In what follows I have drawn on G. Theissen, "Die Legitimitätskrise des Helfens und der barmherzige Samariter: Ein Versuch die Bibel diakonisch zu lesen", in G. Röckle, ed., *Diakonische Kirche – Sendung, Dienst, Leitung: Versuche einer theologischen Orientierung*, Neukirchen-Vluyn, Neukirchener Verlag, 1990, pp.46-76.
[5] Cf. Lev. 19:18. In *Test. Iss.* 7:6f. and *Test. Dan.* 5:3, however, the formula for the neighbour is close to the formula for God.
[6] On the social status of priests and Levites see E. Linnemann, *Gleichnisse Jesus: Einführung und Auslegung*, Göttingen, Vandenhoeck & Ruprecht, 1964, p.144, n.7.

Revelation 12

PETRA VON GEMUNDEN

The biblical text before us is an apocalyptic text from the Revelation to John, full of images, figures and allusions which are not easy to decode. We have difficulty deciphering this text not only because we do not share the ideas and images characteristic of the environment in which it was written, but also because we do not know the particular situation in which it was conceived. Several of the images in Revelation have an aggressive tinge, in which we sense the fear of one who feels threatened. This is why it has often been suggested that Revelation was written in a situation of persecution, more precisely during the persecutions in Asia Minor under the Emperor Domitian (A.D. 90-95). In this context, Revelation would have been intended as a veiled attack against the Roman empire, or as consolation for the communities under threat.

But recent studies have tended to show that the negative image of Domitian is the result of hostile propaganda of that time, not necessarily reflective of what actually happened in Asia Minor. It is thus possible to see the Revelation to John as a true prophecy, the lucid and clairvoyant work of a Christian who recognized that the totalitarian pretensions of the Roman emperor could not be reconciled with the honour due the Lord Jesus. And there were in fact bloody persecutions 100 to 200 years later, just as the visionary of Patmos had predicted. Under Domitian, in any case, there was no systematic persecution, and certainly no omnipresent threat hanging over the lives of Christians.[1]

This situation in the Christian communities, far less dramatic than has typically been supposed, also helps us to understand the letters to the seven churches in Revelation 2 and 3. The tone of these is noticeably different from the main body of the book, which is more clearly apocalyptic (Rev. 4-22).[2] Thus one can expect to find in these letters indications of the actual life of the community. Study of them gives the impression that the author of Revelation is not dealing with a conflict between the churches and an exterior force such as the Roman empire, but rather with an internal community conflict. There are Christians who (according to the author) adapt themselves too easily to the society around them, for example by sharing meals with non-Christian business partners, which almost necessarily implies eating meat which has been sacrificed to idols, and by doing business to make a profit like everybody else. Here, at the level of economic life, it becomes clear what these Christians' fundamental sin is, at which John aims his polemic.

Two negative female figures – the prophetess Jezebel (Rev. 2) and the great whore Babylon (Rev. 17) – are set over against the positive female figure at the centre of the text of Revelation 12: the heavenly woman who gives birth in the presence of a dragon. The contrast between these figures casts light on the issue about which the author is speaking.

Jezebel

In the letter to the church in Thyatira, we read: "But I have this against you: you tolerate that woman Jezebel, who calls herself a prophet and is teaching and beguiling my servants to practise fornication and to eat food sacrificed to idols... Beware, I am throwing her on a bed, and those who commit adultery with her I am throwing into great distress, unless they repent; and I will strike her children dead" (Rev. 2:20,22). The prophetess whom John is attacking here was certainly not named Jezebel. This name recalls the wife of King Ahab in the Old Testament. According to 1 Kings 16:31-33, she was a non-Israelite who seduced King Ahab, led the people to begin to worship Baal, and persecuted Elijah the prophet of God. To call the prophetess in Thyatira Jezebel serves to stigmatize her for her openness to that which is foreign and a threat to "true" religion.

John's concrete reproach is that she teaches the servants of God to "practise fornication and to eat food sacrificed to idols". Probably the reproach of fornication did not have principally to do with sexual behaviour. Already the Old Testament used fornication as a metaphor for turning away from God and towards other gods. The suspicion that foreign cults then led worshippers into sexual orgies served to discredit them even more. John's reproach to the prophetess Jezebel thus did not concern sexual morality, but rather her leaning towards pagan society, including its religious practices.[3]

The subject of eating food sacrificed to idols is one that Paul discussed extensively in 1 Corinthians. This was an issue of basic concern for the early Christians, since almost all available meat came from pagan ritual slaughtering. This is why John describes it as food sacrificed to idols. First-century business contracts were usually negotiated and concluded during meals. Thus entering into and maintaining business relations required accepting invitations to eat together with others. Meetings of craftsmen, merchants, bankers and office-holders were also organized as dinners. Active participation in social, business and political life thus inevitably included sharing in meals,[4] at which it was quite likely that the meat served had been sacrificed to idols. In Corinth there were Christians whom Paul called "the strong", who could eat food which had been sacrificed to idols in the knowledge that there is only one God and one Lord Jesus Christ, and that the idols to whom the meat has been sacrificed do not exist (1 Cor. 8:4-6). These Christians, like the 2nd-century Gnostics, had no problem in eating food sacrificed to idols, because they thought they could not contract any defilement in this way.[5]

John also stigmatizes the knowledge of the followers of Jezebel – "what some call 'the deep things of Satan'" (Rev. 2:24). Jezebel and her followers apparently fit into that "Gnostic" current in which it was considered unnecessary to cut all ties with the pagan environment, which was inevitably marked by the pagan religion: simply knowing that idols do not exist and that worship of the emperor is vanity made them strong enough. This knowledge raised them inwardly above such things, making it unnecessary to fear and avoid all contact with the non-Christian outside world.

This life choice and understanding of life John found frightening. The Old Testament had already compared the activities of merchants to prostitution. For example, Isaiah 23:17 says of Tyre: "she will return to her profession, and will prostitute herself with all the kingdoms of the world on the face of the earth".[6] To do business, to make a profit, is like prostitution. This metaphor is important to John. It is probably no accident that the communities John attacks are precisely the rich ones – unlike Smyrna, which is a poor community and against which he finds nothing negative to say. To make a profit, to engage in trade, is not possible without a certain openness to the Roman empire, that is, to pagan practices which extend into daily life, such as sharing a meal. This is what is meant by Revelation 13:17: "so that no one can buy or sell who does not have the mark (of the beast)".

Babylon

The second negative feminine figure, the great whore Babylon of Revelation 17-18, helps us to understand more precisely John's struggle and his intentions. The great whore Babylon represents the *Dea Roma*, the goddess Rome. The meaning of Babylon is not limited to Rome itself, but extends to every place where the spirit of Rome holds sway.[7] Even through the negative lenses of Revelation, the impression comes through that the prostitute is an attractive and appealing woman. She is "clothed in purple and scarlet, and adorned with gold and jewels and pearls, holding in her hand a golden cup" – and here John clearly adds his negative judgment: "a golden cup full of abominations and the impurities of her fornication" (17:4). The attractiveness of this seductive prostitute recalls the letters to the churches, which show that the Christians who followed the prophetess Jezebel are in the majority.

John says that this woman is "sitting on a scarlet beast that was full of blasphemous names" (17:3). She is astride a power hostile to God; she is riding on Satan. She has close relations with kings and with trade: "the kings of the earth have committed fornication with her, and the merchants of the earth have grown rich from the power of her luxury" (18:3). Thus it is not surprising that it is the kings and the merchants who lament over the fall of Babylon: "And the kings of the earth, who committed fornication and lived in luxury with her, will weep and wail over her..." (18:9; cf. 11-19).

The amplitude of the description of the fate of merchants, shipmasters and seafarers in verses 11-19 leads one to think that John is especially targeting business.[8] The fall of Babylon, the fall of the Roman empire, is seen primarily as an economic collapse. For John, the boundaries are clear: Christians should not have intercourse with Babylon, they should not make common cause with the Roman empire and its trade. To the contrary: John calls on Christians to be set apart, to isolate themselves, to refuse to participate in this system: "Come out of her [Babylon], my people, so that you do not take part in her sins, and so that you do not share in her plagues" (18:4).[9]

Through these two women – Jezebel and the great whore – John attacks those who turn towards the outside world, who adapt themselves to the economic and political milieu and profit from it. To these two women, John announces God's judgment: Jezebel will be thrown onto a bed of distress, and her children will be struck dead. The great whore will be left desolate and naked; her flesh will be devoured and burned with fire (17:16; cf. 18:8).

The woman from heaven

Over against these two negative female figures, John portrays in the myth of chapter 12 a positive female figure: the woman from heaven. This heavenly woman is not luxuriously dressed like the great prostitute, but rather is "clothed with the sun, with the moon under her feet, and on her head a crown of twelve stars" (Rev. 12:1). She is not astride a ferocious beast, but rather is *face to face* with one, a great dragon red as fire. Thus this woman from heaven does not make common cause with the world, but has chosen the good side. She certainly represents the Christians, the community, the church opposed to the negative world. The woman is pregnant, she is enduring birth pangs (12:2), she wishes to give birth to life (bringing life into the world), but the destroying dragon stands before her, "so that he might devour her child as soon as it was born" (12:4).

However, her son, the one "who is to shepherd all the nations with a rod of iron", is saved by God and taken up to his throne (12:5). As for the woman, she "fled into the desert, where she has a place prepared by God, so that there she can be nourished... for a time" (12:6,14). Even though it has already been determined in heaven that God will conquer, the dragon continues to attack the woman and her descendants.

Unlike the negative female figures, the woman from heaven brings life – she is giving birth to salvation. She is face to face with the dragon who continues to attack her as well as her descendants, even though, from God's point of view, God has already secured the victory. The woman flees into the desert – the place of liberation, out of which the people of Israel entered the Promised Land. In the desert, she receives nourishment, like the people of Israel in the days after their flight from Egypt, and like Elijah in the days of his opposition to Jezebel and the prophets of Baal.

In the desert, far from the city and its customs – there is survival in isolation – God personally takes care of God's people, despite those who pursue them. Dressed in the stars of the sky, rather than in earthly luxury drenched in blood, the woman brings forth a life that will bear witness to the saving will of God, which will endure. The life of luxury linked to the beast and the political and economic powers has already been overcome in heaven (12:7ff.) and will soon be annihilated on earth. While the children of Jezebel will be struck dead (Rev. 2:23), the child born in agony and in danger will live.

* * *

These three women illuminate two concepts of the Christian life. On one hand we have a stream of apparently "strong" Christians, who do not equate Christianity with cutting one's ties to the outside world. Their certainty that the Roman empire and its daily manifestations are not God gives them the liberty to turn (with their inward knowledge) towards the outside world and to take meals together with non-Christians – even without any guarantee that the food they are eating has not been sacrificed to idols. They are also free as Christians to engage in trade within the Roman empire; and it is quite possible that there were Christians who had considerable success as traders, who were "rich" (Rev. 3:17).[10]

On the other hand, we have John's conviction that there can be no possible compromise. To eat with non-Christians – in other words, live one's life in the political and economic context of the day – is idolatry; to engage in trade is the equivalent of prostitution. For John, there is only one solution: to give up luxury and instead put on the light from above, to leave the city and all the negative ties to live set apart in the desert, fed and protected by God. In contrast to Jezebel, who had a family (2:23) and thus represents a life more adapted and "bourgeois", even though she is thoughtful and aware of Christ as her Saviour, John represents the ascetic who cuts all ties with the existing society, considering it hostile towards God. John had no family; he was probably an itinerant preacher who had left everything behind in order to devote his entire life to God.

So here are two poles, two choices of a Christian life. Which is the right one? How should we live? Must these two alternatives exclude one another? Under what conditions would they be mutually exclusive? Are there options in between? Can other possibilities be imagined? Which ones, and in what situations?

NOTES

[1] See P. Prigent, "Au temps de l'apocalypse III: Pourquoi les persécutions?", *RPHR*, vol. 55, 1975, pp.341-63.
[2] Cf. H.-J. Klauck, "Das Sendschreiben nach Pergamon und der Kaiserkult in der Johannesoffenbarung", *Biblica*, Rome, Pontificio Istituto Biblico, vol. 73, 1992, pp.153-82.
[3] *Ibid.*, p.167.
[4] E. Schüssler-Fiorenza, "Religion und Politik in der Offenbarung des Johannes", in *Biblische Randbermerkungen: Festschrift R. Schnackenburg*, Würzburg, Echter, 1974, pp.261-72.
[5] Irenaeus, *Against Heretics*, 1,6,3.
[6] Cf. "Tyre as a Type for Rome in Revelation 18", in J. Nelson Kraybill, *Imperial Cult and Commerce in John's Apocalypse*, Sheffield, Sheffield Academic Press, 1996, pp.152-61.
[7] There was a temple to *Dea Roma* in Pergamum; cf. S.R.F. Price, *Rituals and Power: The Roman Imperial Cult in Asia Minor*, Cambridge, Cambridge U.P., 1984, pp.56,133,252.
[8] See Kuno Füssel, *Im Zeichen des Monstrums: Zur Staatskritik der Johannes-Apokalypse*, *Theologie acktuell*, no. 5, Fribourg, Ed. Exodus, 1986, pp.48f.
[9] Kraybill, *op. cit.*, pp.22f.
[10] Written about the same time, the Acts of the Apostles offers a completely different perspective from that of Revelation, speaking with a certain pride that among the Christians are also rich and influential people. The first convert in Europe was Lydia, "a dealer in purple cloth" from Thyatira (Acts 16:14). Purple was a precious product (cf. Rev. 18:12); Thyatira, Lydia's home city, is where "Jezebel" was influential (Rev. 2:20).

How Sustainable Is the Present Project of World Trade?

LUKAS VISCHER

Two unreconciled perspectives

Two discourses about the future of society are predominant today. On the one side, there is continual talk about sustainability or sustainable development. Society and economy must be organized in such a way that the quality of life of future generations will not be impaired. On the other side, there is the vision of a world society in which production, commerce and consumption are increasingly carried out on a global scale without regard for national boundaries.

Neither discourse is limited to academic considerations. Both call for immediate political action. Since the Earth Summit in Rio de Janeiro in 1992, the goal of sustainability is being pursued through a complicated network of intergovernmental negotiations to ensure that certain limits are respected – at least in selected areas of concern such as climate change and biodiversity. The vision of worldwide commerce is the declared theme and purpose of the World Trade Organization (WTO).

But these two perspectives have unequal power. While the demands of sustainability meet with almost insurmountable obstacles, the vision of worldwide commerce has become a project enthusiastically pursued. Sustainability may be widely discussed, but these discussions seem to have limited impact on the actual course of things.

For all who are concerned with the increasing threats to the quality of life on the planet the pressing question arises: How can true sustainability be achieved? Can it be achieved at all within the framework of the present project of society? Or will the demands made in the name of sustainability remain unfulfilled as long as the present direction remains unchanged?

Doubts increase. Today, the "process of globalization" is no longer discussed exclusively by experts but is receiving more and more attention from the general public.[1] Usually this public attention focuses on the social costs of the process. But doubts also arise from an increasing recognition that the present project of society cannot meet the demands of sustainability. Rather than reducing threats to the environment it contributes to the acceleration of its deterioration.

The social price of globalization

The term "globalization" is used today in so many senses that misunderstandings can easily arise. Often the word simply refers in a general way to the factors, events and processes which lead to an ever more encompassing connectedness of humanity. This kind of globalization has been taking place for centuries. Stage by stage borderlines and distances have been overcome and people have been connected. In recent years this process has been accelerated by new and unexpected technological achievements. A world has come into existence where in principle an exchange between all parts of humanity can take place.

In its narrower and more precise meaning, "globalization" refers to the vision of a worldwide market uninhibited by national boundaries and other barriers. In contrast to *inter-* and *multinationalization, globalization* is a new phenomenon. As long as the exchange of goods is carried out between individual states and the sovereign national states remain the actors of commerce we speak of *internationalization*. In the course of the last few centuries, commerce has increasingly been internationalized. A new phenomenon is *multinationalization*, the interpenetration of national economic systems through transnational initiatives for the exploitation of resources, production and commerce. More and more the principal actors are the multinational corporations. *Globalization* goes a step further. Through binding intergovernmental agreements, space should be created for the free competition of economic forces within a single global market. National economic systems should be placed within a larger common framework which will make it possible to maximize production and consumption in a new way.[2]

Globalization in the more general sense of the term is the precondition of this project. Without the ever-closer connection among people the idea of a worldwide market could not have been conceived. Without the technological achievements of the last decades, especially in the areas of mobility and telecommunication, the project would be unable to function. Globalization in the narrower sense of the term is the response to the new context which has arisen. Through its emphasis on production and consumption it contributes in turn to further accelerate the process.

The protagonists of globalization affirm that this new development has already brought considerable gains to humanity. In the space of a few years the liberalization of commerce has raised the volume of international commerce and strengthened at least certain national economic systems; and several countries have registered impressive economic growth. Many countries which previously had to rely on agricultural production have now begun to participate in the industrial development and thus to share in the wealth which it generates. The old dictum that the rising tide will lift all boats, both large and small, seems to be borne out. While the reconstruction of society made necessary by the process of globalization has also caused considerable disadvantages and losses, these are, on this view, only temporary. The promising signs on the horizon justify the expectation that globalization will on the whole turn out to be blessing for all.

But the balance-sheet is in fact far from being clear-cut. Many aspects obviously contradict these claims and give rise to questions and concerns about the negative impact of globalization.

In the first place, globalization aggravates the problem of unemployment. Driven by the laws of competitiveness, firms are obliged to rationalize their production and to achieve the highest possible output with a minimum of workers. Almost daily we hear of mergers of firms – and soon thereafter the inevitable reduction of jobs. While globalization is not the only reason for this development, it is certainly a major contributing factor.

Another consequence is the weakening of nation-states. The initiative increasingly lies with economic forces which are transnationally organized. Their decisions and actions confront governments with *faits accomplis*. Governments are thus forced to form alliances with the real actors of the economic development. To make sure of having a share in the expected rise of economic growth, they seem to have no other choice than to adapt to the demands of economy and to create the best possible conditions for the competitiveness of the firms relevant for their country. Social legislation inevitably suffers in this process. Political control of globalized economy is not yet in sight. The world which results from the process of globalization is highly vulnerable. The Asian crisis shows how easily even seemingly successful economies can experience serious damage.

In the third place, the distribution of the wealth created by increased production is uneven. While the economic situation has considerably improved in certain countries, the prospects for other countries are far from bright. Especially the least developed countries are unable to participate successfully in a world governed by the laws of competitiveness; and there is little reason to expect the mere mechanisms of the market to improve their situation in the near future.

In this perspective the very term globalization is misleading. Though all nations are affected by its consequences, the process cannot really be called "global", since it is dominated by the three economic powers of the United States, Europe and Japan. There are good reasons for speaking of "triadization" rather than globalization. Within the process a struggle for hegemony is taking place. Competition touches not only the spheres of production and commerce but also the question of who will exercise economic and therefore political hegemony in the world.

The scientific and technological developments of the last several decades have resulted in far-reaching changes, calling into question the inherited shape of society and shaking the foundations on which human community has been built. Cultural values with deep roots in history begin to lose their plausibility. New "global" values are being transported into all corners of the planet, resulting in a superficially unified culture. In response, close-knit cultural groups are being formed – based on a variety of ethnic, national and religious traditions. Globalization accentuates and accelerates this double development. True, society has never been a static reality; changes are inevitable and need to be coped with. Today, however, the question arises whether the spiritual resources are available to deal with the rapid change of life conditions.

The ecological price

What about the impact of the globalization process on sustainability and its demands?

The general assumption is that the requirements for sustainability and the process towards uninhibited worldwide trade are compatible or at least not mutually exclusive. Through appropriate measures the construction of the single market can be made sustainable. By coining and promoting the now fashionable term "sustainable development" the Brundtland report and later the United Nations Conference on Environment and Development (UNCED) turned the compatibility of the two discourses into a kind of axiom. What is required to achieve sustainability are only corrections of the growth-oriented economic system. Sustainability can be reached through technological efficiency, international agreements and increased international solidarity.

But many factors give rise to doubts about this thesis. The general trend towards exploitation and destruction has scarcely diminished. True, there has been improvement in some areas. Especially the richer countries have made noticeable progress in such areas as protection against water and air pollution, recycling certain forms of waste and biological agriculture. But despite these partial achievements the general picture is far from reassuring. The progress achieved does not make up for the increase of threats in other areas. There is no need to enumerate these at length: catchwords like "water supply", "rain forests", "biodiversity", "the ozone layer", "climate change", "population growth" are sufficient to remind us of the magnitude of the continuing challenge.

Let me nevertheless elaborate briefly four illustrations of the profound tension between the demands of sustainability and the project of globalization:

1. *Motorized mobility.* After modest beginnings in the first decades of the century motorized mobility on the roads and in the air has expanded by leaps and bounds since the second world war. In recent years a further expansion has set in as it has conquered the countries of the South. In a few years the number of cars in Korea, for instance, has multiplied by ten. According to present estimates the number of vehicles in the world will increase from 500 million today to 2.3 billion in 2030. At the same time air traffic is systematically being built up. Thus the contribution of motorized mobility to carbon dioxide emission is likely to increase steadily in the coming few decades, at least as long as no "clean" or "cleaner" substitutes for gasoline or kerosene are found.

Mobility has always been a driving force in the expansion of trade. The extent of mobility also determines the extent of commerce. The precondition for the expansion of international trade has been the increase and the enormous acceleration of international transport and worldwide telecommunication.[3]

But is such an amount of motorized mobility sustainable? In my view the protagonists of expanded world trade have no answer to this question. They would argue that only a small part of global carbon dioxide emissions are due to the exchange of goods, and that measures of reduction would thus not yield substantial gains. But the issue is not only how many tons of oil are burned by boats, lorries and airlines in the service of international trade. The question is rather the amount of emissions caused by the whole project of accelerated trade. There is little doubt that the combination of intensified mobility and intensified trade gives birth to a dynamism which constitutes a threat to sustainability.

2. *Energy prices and ecological incentives.* In many countries environmentalists promote the idea that market mechanisms could achieve a substantial reduction of today's wasteful use of energy. The price of energy should be increased and taxes levied on the use of fossil fuels. These higher prices will serve as an incentive to reduce energy consumption by introducing more efficient technologies or other economy measures.

The main obstacle to this widely accepted idea is of a political nature. How can a majority be found in favour of higher prices? Such measures will appear both to individual consumers and to industry as economic loss. Individual nations will hesitate voluntarily to deprive themselves of an economic advantage and reduce their competitiveness in international trade. An increase in energy prices could be achieved only through a simultaneous international initiative.

But the World Trade Organization is far from even considering such a step; indeed, the general trend is in the opposite direction. As states abandon their monopolies on energy production and distribution, it is not only objects and services produced by energy but energy itself which becomes a tradable commodity. The laws of competition lead almost inevitably to a lowering of the prices. The privatization of the energy market is being promoted today on the basis of the argument that energy will become cheaper for the individual consumer.

3. *The dangers of accelerated change.* Ever more rapid change is a characteristic of the present period of history. In the past few decades science and technological research have led to an explosion of knowledge. Limits which once seemed unsurpassable have been transcended by epoch-making discoveries. These have not only affected inherited modes of life and modified the structures of society but have also fundamentally changed the relationship of humans to nature. The new knowledge and the capacities resulting from it lead to claims that nature cannot in the long run satisfy. Over-exploitation of natural resources and destruction of the environment are the inevitable consequence. These developments have blinded human beings to the life of nature. Like an impermeable wall, the technological means which humans have created prevents them from perceiving creation in its own dignity. They are not even aware of the damages they cause around them.

The prerequisite for a softer relationship with creation is a new sense of time. Changes in society require time. A new equilibrium cannot be achieved overnight, but needs to be put to the test. The ecological crisis has demonstrated the significance of the precautionary principle. The expectation that nature will absorb any human intervention has turned out to be a naive illusion. The environment is by far more vulnerable than we have assumed so far. Ecological responsibility obliges us therefore to exercise more precaution. To avoid excessive strain a slowing down of the processes of change is required.

The period we live in, however, is one of accelerated developments. Science is forced by the laws of competition to make new discoveries. New technological inventions are thrown on the market, and before humanity has adapted to one new situation it is already confronted with newer challenges. The economic dimension is decisive in this process. Science and technology are more and more in the service of economic gains. Economic success requires making new insights and products available before others are able to take advantage of them. The economic competition has a dimension of time. Every lead pays off. Globalization accelerates this process. As competition acquires global dimensions the struggle for advantages in time further increases. Coping with consequences becomes a secondary consideration.

4. *Intergovernmental conventions.* The hope of the Earth Summit in Rio de Janeiro (1992) was that the community of nations, by adopting a series of binding intergovernmental conventions, would agree to respect certain limits in exploiting nature. Two conventions – on climate change and on biodiversity – were signed in Rio; further desiderata were formulated in the long list of the Agenda 21.

The necessity for binding international agreements to overcome the ecological crisis is widely recognized. But Agenda 21 has been promoted only half-heartedly in recent years. Work on further conventions has had only limited success, and the negotiations on the implementation of the conventions signed at Rio and ratified by a large number of nations have run into impasses. The Conference of Parties to the Convention on Climate Change in Kyoto (December 1997), for instance, was unable to reach a satisfactory agreement on the reduction of carbon dioxide emissions. More daring decisions would not have been credible anyway because the majority of industrialized nations had not honoured even their promise at Rio to reduce the emissions to 1990 levels by the year 2000. If no unexpected change occurs, carbon dioxide emissions are likely to *increase* in the coming years.

Can change be expected in the framework of the present project of worldwide trade? The World Trade Organization has established a Committee on Trade and Environment, but it is no surprise that this body is seen as an element alien to the WTO, with little impact on its work.

The reason for this is that the WTO pursues priorities other than Agenda 21. Agreements which set or seem to set limits to production, trade and consumption contradict the spirit of free competition which underlies the project of globalization. They will be combatted at all levels in the name of competitiveness. Again and again the thesis is defended that the conservation of resources and protection of the environment in general can safely be left to the mechanisms of the world market.[4]

Intergovernmental agreements in the areas of social justice and ecological responsibility can only be realized if a new general consciousness is born which will give rise to new political will.[5]

Can the present development be mastered? Can sustainability be achieved through corrective measures?[6] Or is a more fundamental reorientation of society needed? Is it possible to introduce the necessary measures so long as they continue to be consistently considered as an afterthought? Is it not unlikely that sustainability will be realized so long as "sustainable" is no more than the adjective qualifying the noun "development"? Does sustainability not need to become the noun determining the model of society to be adopted?

Possible reorientations

Proposals seeking to meet the criterion of sustainability seem to point in two directions:

1. *The recognition of scales.* The first starts from the recognition that natural resources are limited and that human economic activities must therefore stay within these limits. Herman Daly has again and again reminded us of the basic insight that the economic system is only a subsystem of the biosystem. He promotes the idea of scale or scales which must not be trespassed.[7] These scales are to be defined in harmony with the rules of balance and capacity of regeneration in the household of nature. In any case, human claims must never go as far as to cause irreversible damage.

The idea of scale rules out the assumption of continuous economic growth. True, estimates made in the 1970s about the availability of resources have proved to be too pessimistic. Natural resources continue to be available to a larger extent than was assumed at that time; and it is likely that for certain resources substitutes can be found. Nevertheless, pressure has increased in several areas, and it remains essential to establish realistic scales to guide economic exploitation. For example, scientists have calculated that per capita emissions of carbon dioxide should not exceed 1.7 tons; and the establishment of maximum limits is of utmost importance in today's disputes among nations over fishing rights.

Closely related to the concept of scale is the suggestion of the need for a limit to human needs and desires. An economic system must not grow beyond a certain point. Both individuals and society as a whole need to be able to declare a certain level of wealth sufficient. Some authors have compared the economic system to the growth of a tree. Growth beyond the height that is characteristic for a particular tree is considered abnormal, perhaps even a sign of cancerous illness. Just as trees are not meant to "grow into heaven", so society should not measure achievement exclusively in terms of economic growth. Instead of maximizing production and consumption, it must be guided by values such as sufficiency, simplicity, care and solidarity.

Bob Goudzwaard and Harry de Lange speak of "a minimal provision for our own basic needs (as well for the basic needs of all), in conjunction with establishing a maximum level of consumption". They advocate in this connection an "economics of enough", which distinguishes "material luxury desires from the legitimate economic needs of people today and of future generations" and gives priority to "meeting economic needs: the needs of the poorest, of those lacking work, of the environment and its sustainability, and of human community. But this reforming of our economic order comes at a price, a price that material desires must pay. In an economics of enough, a society must be willing to accept that general income increases... will gradually come to an end."[8]

2. *The significance of regions.* The second proposal emphasizes the need for organizing the economy and society in general in smaller units. Instead of thinking primarily in terms of worldwide relations, we should give greater value to the role of the local community.

The arguments for this orientation vary. For many, the quality of human relations is the primary concern. Though recognizing how repressive small communities can be, they hold that human community must manifest itself primarily in small units, where the sense of civic responsibility and cultural particularities can flourish. But the primary argument is that of sustainability. Resources will be more wisely used when exploitation, production and consumption take place within limited geographical areas. In addition, the need for motorized mobility of persons and goods will be reduced.

This is not of course a call for autarky. Many problems today transcend the competence of a region and require international agreement. Given the inequalities of regions, international commerce is indispensable. The issue is what place local and regional communities will be given within the framework of the international community. The protagonists of "decentralization" promote the view that the local community should be both the starting point and the goal of any order of society. They often speak of the worldwide society as a "community of communities".

Herman E. Daly and John B. Cobb argue that

> it is folly to sacrifice existing institutions of community at the national level in the supposed service of non-existent institutions of community at the world level. Better to build and strengthen the weakening bonds of national community first, and then expand community by federation into larger trading blocs among national communities that have similar community standards regarding wages, welfare, population control, environmental protection, and conservation. True efficiency lies in the protection of these hard-won community standards from the degenerative competition of individualistic free trade, which comes to rest only at the lowest common denominator.[9]

Cobb portrays a sustainable society as "decentralized". Human needs should be met locally "as far as possible, depending on trade only when necessary". Only as local communities regain basic control over their own economies can there be health in human community and an effective community of people within the larger environment of living things. Further, it is only by this radical decentralization that dependence on an exhaustible supply of energy can be overcome.[10]

Similarly, Larry Rasmussen seeks to give the classical notion of subsidiarity a contemporary meaning: "Subsidiarity means that what can be accomplished on a smaller scale at close range by high participation with available resources should not be given over to, or allowed to be taken over by, larger and more distant organizations."[11] The guideline is not what is the most "local" but what is the *appropriate* level of organization and response, for "in a world of maldistributed resources and power, the local cannot be the only locus of responsible action, just as it is not the only place we meet and live together... The necessary guideline is not 'no trade' or 'no markets' or even 'minimal trade' and minimal markets'. The guideline is to minimize the appropriation of carrying capacity from elsewhere, thus risking other people's and otherkind's lives in the present and for the future."[12]

The unresolved conflict

As reasonable as such considerations and theses may sound, there can be no doubt that the dynamism of present developments points in exactly the opposite direction.

How can a society geared to continuous growth start being guided by scales? Scarcities may arise which require limitations in the use of resources in certain areas. But such situations will be interpreted primarily as a call to redress the situation by deploying new creativity. From where could the readiness come to be content with a certain level of consumption? The conviction that human desires are in principle unlimited is deeply rooted in Western culture, and because it serves the interests of the present system it is vigorously promoted at all levels of society. Having transcended the boundaries of space and time, how can human beings find their way back to an emphasis on the local community? The weakness of all the scenarios proposed for achieving a transition from here to there lies in their inability to show how the will for change can develop under present circumstances.[13]

The dynamic force of present processes is so strong that movements of opposition seem to have little chance. The consensus on which it relies seems so evident that it can be presented as the only realistic course. Proposals in other directions can be dismissed as nostalgia, romantic dreams or idealistic programmes, of academic interest perhaps, but not applicable in reality.

So what sense does it make to conduct the debate at this level? Instead of getting lost in speculations, is it not better to limit the discussion to possible corrections of the present course? If real solutions are out of reach, is it not better to make the present development if not sustainable, at least more nearly sustainable? Green parties and environmental NGOs are faced with this dilemma. In debates on economy and society they are often obliged to defend positions which do not correspond to their deepest convictions and concerns but fit into the framework of present debates.

But all this leaves many people with a deep malaise. In the depth of their hearts they are aware of the contradictions in which they live and operate. They realize that sustainability demands more drastic measures than simple corrections, but they know that their views will not be heeded. Though it is obvious that the present course cannot fulfil the demands of sustainability, no alternatives can be pursued.

Motorized mobility provides a good illustration of this split consciousness. Though its negative consequences are evident, even environmentalists hesitate to propose measures for its reduction. Instead, debate focuses on possible corrections: technological improvements of vehicles, internalization of external costs into the price of gasoline, shifting traffic from road to rail.

We are thus living in two worlds. There is on the one hand the desire to live in a world in which human beings live in harmonious communion with the created world. Poets, film-makers and intellectuals of all kinds make this their theme. They articulate a pain deep in our hearts. On the other hand decisions are taken which confirm and push further present trends.

The ideological dimension

Why does the vision of a world society knit together by bonds of trade exercise so much fascination? Why is it so difficult even to imagine a different course?

In the first place, the process can rely on the power of historical developments. While sustainability represents a new orientation, the project of globalization can build on history. The expansion of trade to world dimensions appears to be the logical next step in the economic history of recent decades and even centuries.

Moreover, this development seems so far to be crowned with success. It has brought wealth – at least to the industrialized world. Despite increasing social problems and the seemingly insurmountable inequality between rich and poor nations, only a very few would advocate a return to earlier levels of wealth and comfort. Science and technology have led to an increase of knowledge and capacities. Science, technology, production, commerce and consumption are now so closely intertwined that the course cannot be changed without the risk of a serious disintegration of society.

There is, furthermore, the history of recent decades, which was dominated by the antagonism of two systems – on the one hand the free interaction of economic forces, on the other hand central control in almost all realms of society. But East and West, though deeply divided in many respects, were ultimately committed to the same goal – to foster through economic growth the welfare of the nations. They sought to prove the superiority of their systems by achieving economic expansion. In the latter years of their confrontation, the economic dimension took on increased significance.

The collapse of the Marxist regimes was primarily an economic collapse. The field was now free. The victorious side now had the task of providing the pattern for a new world order. It was almost inevitable to rely on the patterns which had guided its economic thinking in the past. The occasion had now come to pursue the Western system on a world basis. How could the West have turned down this opportunity?

As important as all these considerations may be, they do not yet provide the full answer. Behind the vision of a worldwide market is an ideological presupposition which has been a guiding concept in the history of the West. It has to do with a particular understanding of the destiny and vocation of human beings and humanity as a whole. Humanity is called to reach, in the course of its history, ever new heights of being human. As knowledge and capacities increase, human beings become more and more the masters of nature. They free themselves from the bonds which once seemed to be imposed on them forever by nature. They achieve greater wealth. Horizons gradually expand. While history is not linear progress and there are failures and catastrophes, the basic vocation of humanity remains unchanged. Ultimately history moves on an ascending line.

This understanding of human history has diverse roots. Arising in the Renaissance, it became dominant in the Western world during the 17th century. Earlier, human beings had primarily been seen as subject to God and God's will. Now they came to consider themselves increasingly as masters of their own history. Whereas the Reformers, even Calvin, thought of human economic life primarily in terms of subsistence and solidarity, the categories of increased wealth and competitivity began to come to the fore.

Closely related to the vision of human self-expansion is the expectation that humanity will gradually grow together into a tangible worldwide unity. Borderlines fall. Separate worlds enter into relation with one another. Cultures increasingly interact. The vision of a world living in peace acquires more and more importance. To be sure, there will also be new conflicts, and because of their worldwide character they will be more murderous than anything previous. But in these conflicts the readiness for new relationships among the nations matures.

The Western world attributed to itself the pioneering role in this process. The power it held through scientific and technological knowledge seemed to destine the West to the particular task of giving birth to the new world. Western nations regarded themselves as called to lead humankind to the goal it had eventually to reach. While the British empire emphasized the cultural vocation of the West, the focus later shifted to the economic development of the nations. President Truman's famous speech in 1946 presented the programme which was to guide political action in the following decades. The economically developed nations had the task of leading the "underdeveloped nations" to new wealth and thus assure peace among the nations. Later, the papal encyclical *Populorum progressio* (1967) would proclaim that "development is the new name for peace".

All these concepts face the same difficulty. How will the transition from present history to the promised land take place? How can it be shown that the fruit of a peaceful and happy world is really maturing in the events of history? How can power come to be shared and a state of responsible community emerge? Immanuel Kant thought he had discovered a "plan of nature" leading to such a state.[14] Marxism believed that history would inexorably create a classless society.

All these expectations of a better future claimed to be based on an "objective" perception of history. No convincing proof of this was ever offered, and the experience of the last decades has made clear that it *could not* be given. The transition from the antagonisms of history to a peaceful world is beyond human capacity. Even the most altruistic messianic movement cannot break out of the game of power and counter-power. Indeed, messianic movements are so easily transformed into powers of exploitation and oppression precisely because they regard themselves as entitled to sacrifice the well-being of the present generation in the name of an allegedly even better future.

Nevertheless, such visionary thinking continues today. Building on the idea of a development encompassing all nations, a new project is being proposed which is meant to bring liberty and wealth to the world. Motifs from the past are being revived: boundaries must be transcended, intensified exchange will create new bonds and reduce violence among nations.

In November 1995, Michel Camdessus, director general of the International Monetary Fund, addressed a group of Roman Catholic intellectuals on the future "global city". Recalling the founding of the United Nations and the Bretton Woods Institutions 50 years earlier he appealed for people "to renew their vision of a better world to be constructed". Two events, he said, have changed the course of history: the fall of the Berlin wall and the rising dynamism of globalization. Both can have enormous consequences for the freedom and the brotherhood of people. They are harbingers of a new order – a unified world and an world economy which provides a home to all.

Are we then on the way to a better world? Camdessus remains prudent. He invokes neither a "plan of nature" nor the "objective course of history". In his eyes the future is open. But he is deeply convinced that the road chosen holds enormous promises. Despite all uncertainties, it is thus worthwhile, even morally required, to engage all our capacities in the project. The experience of present instability must not deter us. We are called to make a wager that these signs are signs of the time, representing a new chance for the world. We have nothing to lose in making this wager, but it does impose on us the obligation to appropriate the ambivalent dynamics and so to direct them that they bring about a more fraternal world.

It is interesting that Camdessus does not speak of certainties but of chances and risks. His élan has its roots in a sort of creed, legitimizing the project of globalization by the imperative of hope. Because human beings are called to higher destinies, doubt and misgivings must be overcome. Support for this project is thus put in moral terms. In those who resist he sees the same "great fear" which made people in the 10th century expect the end of the world in the year 1000.[15]

In the face of such ideological convictions, speaking of scales can only be interpreted as a step backward and emphasizing the significance of local communities as a betrayal of the true vocation of humankind. The only true road forward is globalization.

The witness of the churches

In this debate do the churches speak a word of warning, pointing to another understanding of the vocation of humankind? Does their thinking represent an alternative? Or do they in fact share the vision of an ever-increasing unity of humankind? Have they perhaps even been a driving force in developing this vision? The picture is ambivalent.

The message of the Christian churches points to the horizon of the whole of humanity. God, the Creator of *all* things, has become human in Jesus Christ. The kingdom, announced by Jesus, brings human history to its end and fulfilment. With the coming of Christ the moment of decision has come for *all* nations. God's grace has been offered to them. "Rejoice, O Gentiles, with his people, and again, praise the Lord, *all* Gentiles, and let *all* the people praise him" (Rom. 15:10-11). The preaching of the apostles is addressed to the whole *oikoumene*, from Jerusalem, to Judaea and Samaria, and to the ends of the earth. The goal is to gather the people before God. All are called to present their lives to God as living sacrifice of praise. There is in this movement an enormous dynamism. Boundaries are transcended. Walls are torn down to make room for the new communion. All who accept the message become living stones in the great temple of God resulting from the proclamation of the good news.

What is the relationship of this Christian vision to the fact that the history of nations more and more merged into one single history of humanity? How is this historical development to be interpreted? What does it mean for Christians that horizons expand; and what is the role of the churches in a world which seems to become steadily smaller?

Christian perspectives have no doubt been a driving force in this development. At the same time, however, the emerging "unity of humankind" presented a formidable challenge to the churches. The church was now called to manifest its true nature. The creed speaks of "one, holy, catholic and apostolic church". Were these new developments not the occasion to give renewed expression to the catholicity of the church? The missionary and later the ecumenical movements have many roots. But there is no doubt that they are in part a response to the historical process of the growing interdependence of humanity. Faced with new horizons, faced with the conflicts arising from the interaction of nations, and above all faced with the mounting impact of empires, the churches had to come together. They had to leave behind their imprisonment within national boundaries and make an exodus into a wider community.

How is the relationship between the church and humankind to be understood? Different answers can be and have been given.[16]

The church may consider itself as the centre of humankind. The proclamation of the gospel brings into existence a community which is called to be a model for the nations, a *societas perfecta* which can serve as source of inspiration. The church anticipates in its own midst the community which the nations are destined to achieve. Its witness thus focuses on pointing – through its existence and through its word – to the sources of true communion. It will denounce deviations and contribute to the sound development of human community.

This self-understanding is particularly alive in the Roman Catholic Church, but it has also played a significant role in the ecumenical movement. Cardinal Ottaviani gave it succinct expression when Pope Paul VI returned from a visit to the United Nations, declaring that the pope had succeeded in showing that the church was to be considered as the "soul of the community of all peoples".

Closer scrutiny shows that such claims cannot be maintained. Far from being a *societas perfecta*, the church is divided. Its being and its witness reflect the conflicts that divide the world. Throughout its history it has identified with the forces which have dominated and determined the process of globalization. It bears the marks of this history; and it would be an illusion to think that it can free itself from it by simply referring to its "spiritual" vocation. The Western world from which the present project of society emanates is, in fact, shaped by the Christian tradition, and the messianic dimension which characterizes it has undeniably Christian roots.

A new manifestation of the catholicity of the church can therefore only be achieved on the basis of radical self-criticism. A conversion and a new departure are required. The church must seek to become free from the identification with its Western origins.

There is, for instance, the question of how to evaluate the efforts of other movements towards worldwide unity. The church is not alone in the process towards closer bonds among the nations. It must recognize that it is part of a larger process, side by side with other forces, both religious and secular, which seek to respond to today's challenges from their perspective. Presumably, the celebration of the year 2000 will show both the pretensions of Christianity and the necessity to transcend them. Unity cannot be constructed by the church alone.

Of even greater importance is the conviction that the place of the church may never be at the side of the powerful. It must identify with the victims of power. Present trends exact an enormous price. Commitment to the gospel requires taking sides with those who have to pay this price. Over the last several decades the churches have gradually been led to new forms of solidarity with people suffering exploitation and oppression. Increasingly, they have not confined their efforts to calling for dialogue and peace and mediating in conflicts, but have sought to strengthen the voice and resistance of the victims of power. Thus, for the sake of *catholicity*, the churches have sought identification with particular interests.

In all this, however, the legitimacy and even the desirability of growing unity among the nations were never called into question. The debate concentrated exclusively on how the conditions for justice and equity could be assured. The churches sought to give a more humane face to the worldwide community. Against violence, injustice and oppression they promoted values such as solidarity, peace and justice.

But today's challenges raise new questions. The process towards unification which has so far been considered the inevitable destiny of humankind needs to be questioned. In fact, already in 1968, one of the first papers written for the WCC study on the Unity of the Church and the Unity of Humankind emphasized the ambivalence of the process towards increasing interdependence, recognizing that this did not necessarily represent a stage on the way to new heights but might be "a stage on the way to self-destruction..., not progress but rather progressing in the uncertainty whether perhaps somewhere ahead bridges have already collapsed".

The ecological crisis reinforces this doubt. Less and less can the possibility of self-destruction be ruled out. Marquis N.C. Condorcet (1743-94), an Enlightenment philosopher who firmly believed in progress, pointed to the contradiction in which we live: "Progress has its only limits in the temporal existence of the planet we have been made dependent on by nature." What he wanted to say was that there were practically no limits. In fact, the limits he identified appear more and more clearly today. Though the very existence of the planet may not be threatened, its capacity to provide humankind with a safe habitat is far from assured. The primary question therefore is not just how to correct the course of developments but how to establish a relationship to God's creation which respects its limits. What has been and continues to be regarded as progress turns out to be a threat to the future.

The churches are far from being of one mind in this respect. Their witness has so far moved within the framework of the dominant ideology. Although they were critical in many respects, they shared its presuppositions even in their criticism. In many circles new perspectives are beginning to be developed. But the real debate within the churches is still ahead.

Theological perspectives

It seems to me that new orientations are needed in at least three areas:

1. *God's wisdom in creation.* In the first place the simple fact needs to emphasize that human beings are part of creation and must therefore respect the limits imposed on them. While they have received the capacity to extend these limits, this basic dependence remains, whatever their achievements. Humanity can come to its fulfilment only in communion with other human beings and with creation as a whole. The fulfilment of human life is not the domination of nature, but wisdom and care in relating to it.

The Bible speaks of wisdom as participating in God's act of creating the world. Wisdom was created before all things and therefore rules in all things. "When God marked out the foundations of the earth, then I was beside God like a master workman, and I was daily God's delight rejoicing before God always, rejoicing in God's inhabited world" (Prov. 8:29-31). The task, therefore, is to discover the ways of wisdom in creation and to follow them. The values presently determining public life – increased output, economic growth, more and more consumption – are certainly not in harmony with the rules of wisdom. Even raising the levels of wealth cannot unquestionably be considered as positive. In the light of wisdom the first consideration needs to be the equilibrium between exploitation and regeneration.

2. *What can humanity reasonably hope for?* Does the Bible really speak of history as an ascending line? Many biblical passages point to the contrary. God's people have been called in a world which is eventually moving to its end. Israel realizes more and more that it is a people among peoples. The horizon widens, especially in the apocalyptic literature. God rules over the whole of humankind. The visions attributed to the prophet Daniel present the history of humankind rather as a descending line. Empires follow one on the other, each one more oppressive and violent than the preceding. The true hope of the people lies beyond human history. Empires will be destroyed – or rather, will destroy themselves – and will make room for God's kingdom. The same picture is seen in the New Testament. Christ's resurrection does not mean that history now moves to new heights. Violence and death do not disappear. The ultimate hope of the church is God's kingdom beyond history. Its contours have become visible in Christ. In communion with him its presence can be anticipated.

It is important to underline this aspect, because Christian hope has often been portrayed as hope within the framework of an ascending human history. Faced with ideologies of all sorts, especially with Marxist speculations about the future, and with the innate human desire for confidence and dynamism, the temptation was almost inevitable to identify historical developments with the beginnings of God's kingdom. History was interpreted as a process leading into God's kingdom, or conversely, God's kingdom was seen as the fruit slowly maturing in the course of human history. But the future of humankind is, to say the least, radically open. As we wait for God's kingdom, we shall do our best to assure conditions which allow living together in justice and peace. Christian hope frees our hearts from the obsession constantly to develop "new visions" of the future. Christian hope enables us to practise a critical pragmatism.

3. *Communion – worldwide and local.* The growing interdependence of humankind is thus not simply to be considered as a gain. Like all historical developments, it is deeply ambivalent. The churches, which have been inclined to view it positively, must develop a more critical assessment. The ecumenical movement has perhaps not always sufficiently seen that the biblical witness points in two directions. On the one hand,

it emphasizes the need for transcending boundaries, for communities to overcome their national, ethnic, cultural, linguistic or religious exclusiveness. Any exclusion of others in the name of preserving one's own identity and defending the narrow interests of one's own community must be resisted.

On the other hand, there is also a recurring criticism of the empires of this world. The fact that God chose Israel, an insignificant people by human standards, shows that God's ways do not correspond to human history, which is dominated by the interaction of great powers. The existence of the particular people Israel is a living critique of imperial claims. The image of the giant statue (Dan. 2) with its feet partly of iron and partly of clay has a firm place in the biblical message. In particular, the biblical texts denounce the temptation of the power resulting from trade. "In the abundance of your trade you were filled with violence and you sinned," Ezekiel says of the king of Tyre (28:16).

From the beginning, the history of the church was characterized by the same critique. By insisting on God's claims the church inevitably came into conflict with the Roman empire. The New Testament leaves no doubt. As history advances human self-assertion becomes more stubborn and aggressive.

This double front implies a twofold witness. The gospel requires on the one hand a critique of all forces of exclusiveness. Too often the churches succumb to the temptation of identifying themselves with particular interests. Sometimes they have even become the driving force and spiritual guarantor of national and other identities. The message of the church points in the direction of the whole *oikoumene*. But this does not mean that all movements towards increased interdependence are to be affirmed. Churches must resist all concentrations of power. Their primary concern will always be the quality of communion in each place. The uniqueness of the notion of catholicity is that it includes both dimensions – the local and the universal. The churches must contribute to a sound interaction between communities at local and universal levels. Thus they also have the task of defending the interests of the local community against the claims of superior universal structures. The test for the quality of a universal order lies in the quality of community in each place.

The obvious threats to which humanity today is exposed would seem to make the direction for the churches clear. On the one hand they must recall the limits which economic expansion has to respect. On the other hand they must struggle for the preservation of responsible societies in each place. These postulates may appear as a new orientation but they in fact have deep roots in the tradition of Christian social teaching. They correspond to the familiar notions of "subsistence" and "subsidiarity". Subsistence raises the issue of real and justifiable human needs within the whole of creation; subsidiarity suggests that, without abandoning universal solidarity, responsibility is to be exercised at the lowest possible level. In my view it is urgent for the churches to revive these notions and to develop them in the context of today's challenges.

* * *

Can the course of history still be changed? There is no clear-cut answer to this question. Much can be said to support the view that present developments cannot be changed. In all probability we have to count with further destruction and loss of quality of life. While the beginnings of a new orientation may be evident, there is still a long way to go before a consensus can be reached on alternative models of society. A new future could arise, but it may also be that it will then be too late to return to healthier forms of society.

NOTES

[1] Cf. the best-seller by Hans-Peter Martin and Harald Schumann, *Die Globalisierungsfalle*, Hamburg, Rowohlt, 1996.
[2] The following two descriptions of this process may serve as illustrations: "Globalization is a process whereby producers and investors increasingly behave as if the world economy consisted of one single market and production area with regional and national sub-sectors, rather than a set of national economies linked by trade and investment flows" (UNCTAD 1996). "The widening of the spectrum of goods and services entering international trade as a consequence of trade liberalization, increased freedom of establishment and technical innovations allowing long-distance delivery of services" (Jones and Kierzkowski).
[3] Daniel Finn writes: "Whether we consider the building of railroads in the US and Canada during the 19th century, the digging of canals in England during the 18th century, or the improvements in transportation brought about by air travel, electronics, and computers in the 20th century, the argument is the same. The mainstream economic view is that when improved transportation allows people to make economic exchanges with others at greater distances – whether across the nation or across the world – there will be more specialization in production, higher productivity, and higher levels of welfare. From the economist's perspective, then, the debate about international trade is about taking advantage of markets that have been extended by technological capacity but restricted by legal intervention"; *Just Trading: On the Ethics and Economics of International Trade*, Nashville, TN, Abingdon, 1996, p.30; cf. p.171.
[4] "We should recognize that market solutions can also be found to ecological concerns (responsible forestry, aided by competitive prices, can help to husband resources, exploitative mining will wear them out). The problem economists have to face is to calculate the costs appropriately" (see below Peter Tulloch, p. 105). According to Finn, "international commerce requires a framework of rules. In most cases these must be rooted both in national legislation and in international agreement. Because of the importance of background assumptions concerning technological optimism in evaluating the depletion of non-renewable resources and of the value of species diversity in assessing prospects for biodiversity, participants to these debates have unusually

wide differences to negotiate in structuring such agreements. Significant progress has been made in the daunting task of establishing a scientifically rigorous definition for global biogeophysical sustainability, but far more work has yet to be done" (*op. cit.*, p.160). The most difficult problem, however, is to introduce the prices once they have been established; there is no answer to this question yet.

[5] The thesis of a series of intergovernmental "contracts" has been coherently defended by The Group of Lisbon under the leadership of Riccardo Petrella. In analogy to developments in the 19th century when at national level in the new context of the industrial era social legislation was introduced there is now need not only for a social but also an environmental contract at the international level. The Group of Lisbon places its hope for the future on non-governmental forces of all kinds. The prerequisites of a promising future are thus the protection and strengthening of democratic rights. Cf. Group of Lisbon, *Limits to Competition*, Cambridge/London, MIT Press, 1995.

[6] In recent years there has been much talk about the ethical dimension of the present challenge. Only on the basis of new "world ethos" will the nascent global society be able to survive. The primary task therefore is to bear witness to fundamental ethical commitments both in politics and in economics. Especially the churches have to contribute to the recognition of universal ethical values. As ethical principles and commitments find general recognition the present system can, even will be transformed into a "responsible society". "Without rules, without traditions, without a minimal ethical consensus our society will collapse as the socialist system has collapsed in recent years" (Marion Gräfin von Doenhoff, *Zivilisiert den Kapitalismus*, 1997, Stuttgart, Dt.-Verl.-Anst., cover page). In his broadly based study *Global Ethics for Global Politics and Economics*, London, SCM, 1997, Hans Küng defends similar ideas. The concern of the book is to formulate a "core of global ethics", i.e. a set of general principles which are to guide both political and economic activities (p.110). Küng does not hope for a perfect world. He seeks a middle way between unrealistic idealism and realism without any ethical convictions. "Both in the sphere of politics and in that of economics we need a new sense of responsibility" (p.277). Although these considerations can hardly be questioned, Küng's book remains unsatisfactory because it relies on a unilateral and superficial analysis. He speaks of globalization as "unavoidable", "ambivalent", "unpredictable" in its consequences but nevertheless "controllable" (pp.160-67). The ecological crisis is hardly mentioned (pp.205f.) and the tensions resulting from it are not dealt with at all. Well-intentioned as Küng's call for ethical principles may be, the book does not really do justice to the present situation.

[7] Daly has also used the striking image of an ecological Plimsoll line of the planet. "The absolute optimal scale of load is recognized in the maritime institution of the Plimsoll line. When the watermark hits the Plimsoll line the boat is full, it has reached its carrying capacity... The major task of environmental macro-economics is to design an economic institution analogous to the Plimsoll mark"; cf. *Sustainable Growth: A Contradiction in Terms?*, Geneva, 1993, pp.41-42.

[8] Bob Goudzwaard and Harry de Lange, *Beyond Poverty and Affluence: Towards an Economy of Care*, Geneva, WCC, 1994, pp.74,78,90; similar theses are put forward by Anna Sax, Peter Haber and Daniel Wiener, *Das Existenz-Maximum*, Zurich, Werdverl., 1997.

[9] Herman E. Daly and John B. Cobb, *For the Common Good: Redirecting the Economy toward Community, the Environment and the Future*, Boston, Beacon, 1989, p.235.

[10] John B. Cobb, *Sustainability*, Maryknoll, NY, Orbis, 1992, p.48.

[11] Larry Rasmussen, *Earth Community, Earth Ethics*, Geneva, WCC, 1996, pp.336f.

[12] *Ibid.*, p.339.

[13] Detailed proposals as to how the economic system could be changed are put forward in the last part of Daly and Cobb, *op. cit.*, and by Goudzwaard and de Lange, who conclude their analysis with a "Twelve Step Programme" for economic recovery (*op. cit.*, pp.134-61).

[14] Immanuel Kant, *Idee zu einer allgemeinen Geschichte in weltbürgerlicher Absicht*, These 8.

[15] In fact there were no exceptional apprehensions in the 10th century about the approaching second millennium; the "great fear" is an invention of the 19th century which, of course, looked condescendingly on the "dark" ages; cf. Lukas Vischer, "Zwei Jahrtausendwenden", in *Theologie auf dem Weg in das dritte Jahrtausend*, Gütersloh, Gütersloher Verl.-Haus, 1996, pp.69ff.

[16] The question of the relationship between the oneness of the church and ever-increasing interdependence of humanity has been a theme of the ecumenical movement from the outset. In the 1960s and 1970s it was the subject of a broadly based study by the World Council of Churches. Cf. Gert Rüppell, *Einheit ist unteilbar: Die Menschheit und ihre Einheit als Thema der ökumenischen Bewegung*, Rothenburg, Ernst Lange Institut, 1992.

Sustainability, Full Employment and Globalization

Contradictions or Complements?

FRANCIS WILSON

Before examining the consequences of globalization for sustainability, let me set the context with an overview of the thinking that emerged from the first two consultations convened by the Visser 't Hooft Fund, in 1993 and 1995.[1]

The first consultation began with the knowledge that reality for this generation has changed in two fundamental ways. For the first time in history, humanity has a sense of the fragility of Spaceship Earth, on which we travel and which now shows numerous signs of becoming full, if not overcrowded. The combination of global population increase with rapid industrialization is clearly creating stresses which were not visible when the world was an emptier place. Reports of holes in the ozone layer above the Antarctic, of massive oil spills destroying miles of fragile marine life along the coast of North America, of acid rain destroying forests in Western Europe, of environmental catastrophes in Eastern Europe, of unbreathable air in the polluted mega-cities of Asia and Latin America, of climatic change due to the effect of carbon dioxide emissions[2] – all these raise troubling questions about the capacity of the planet to absorb the high and rising levels of population and material production which have now been reached. These questions are compounded by the realization that resources once seen as indestructible are indeed vanishing. Topsoil itself continues to erode at a rate which, in some parts of the world, threatens people's capacity to grow food or sustain life as they once did; tropical rain forests are being cut down much faster than they are being replanted; thousands of species are becoming extinct each year. Water itself is increasingly seen as a finite and vulnerable resource.

Against this background the first consultation defined sustainability as a condition "which leaves the world as rich in resources and opportunities as it inherited" – meaning "that renewable resources are consumed no faster than they can be renewed, that non-renewable resources are consumed no faster than renewable substitutes can be found, that wastes are discharged at a rate no greater than they can be processed by nature or human devices".

The possible contradictions inherent in pursuing the double goal of sustainability and growth raise a no less difficult question, which the next workshop took up: if growth must be curtailed because of its damaging consequences to the planet, can this be done in a way that does not harm whatever prospects there are for reducing, if not eliminating, the widespread poverty and particularly the growing levels of unemployment? To put it another way, if "sustainable growth" is a contradiction in terms, is there not an even more fundamental contradiction embedded in the second reality of widespread unemployment in many different parts of the world where the only solution appears to be yet more economic growth? Thus the second consultation examined the apparent conflict between policies deemed necessary for dealing with environmental degradation and policies appropriate for reducing the unemployment and marginalization found in so many parts of the world.

The conflict between development including economic growth and the environment seems particularly acute during the early stages of industrialization, whether in Europe in the 19th century or in Asia at the end of the 20th:

> In not turning its attention to environmental problems until certain basic material conditions have been fulfilled, China [for example] is no different from other countries that have already walked the path of primary industrialization. The difficult question is whether or not the very much larger absolute population numbers with which Beijing or Bombay or indeed the world as a whole has to cope in the 1990s, compared with Paris or Pittsburgh in earlier generation, fundamentally alters the possibility of a successful outcome from an environmental perspective.[3]

Florence Ziumbe of Zimbabwe helped this consultation to see that the debate must go beyond sustainability, growth and work to include the impact of globalization as it is manifested in externally imposed Structural Adjustment Programmes and the process of tariff reduction. "Trade liberalization", she wrote, "as currently being implemented in Zimbabwe and many countries in Africa creates an impediment to the achievements of sustainable development."[4]

Mariama Williams, an economist from the State University of New York, reflected insightfully on some of the possible consequences of the then recently established World Trade Organization (WTO). Her paper drew attention to the failure of rich countries to deal with the shackling effect of the debt crisis and of the dangers of globalization, as furthered by the WTO, leading not only to negative fallout for labour but also to a backtracking on environmental issues.[5]

* * *

What is globalization? In what follows I shall try to provide some perspectives on this question from the developing world – in my case southern Africa.

Essentially, globalization may be understood as the increasing interaction, primarily through trade and communication, of all parts of the world. At one level there is nothing new about this. The history of trade is also the history of widening globalization.

But where does one start? Should our analysis begin with the consequences of Portuguese explorers, like Vasco da Gama, looking for trade routes at the end of the 15th century? Or with the impact of the entrepreneurs of the Dutch East India Company, consolidating their trade routes in the middle of the 17th century? Or with imperialists of the British empire, seeking to ensure both supplies of raw materials and markets for their industrial products?

Here I shall begin in the 19th century, where two examples can help us to see immediately that whether "trade" is good or bad depends on the circumstances.

The first example is the Corn Laws, which established barriers to the import of wheat into Britain. These were abolished at the end of the 1840s after the Irish famine, opening the doors of the British Isles to imports of wheat from the United States and dramatically lowering the price of food. In fact there was a huge expansion of European trade in the 19th century, both within countries such as Germany and Italy as political unification created favourable conditions for trade, and between countries and continents.

But even this expansion was not without ambiguities. A.G. Kenwood and A.L. Lougheed, after describing the enormous opening up of trade in Europe from the end of the Napoleonic wars until about 1880, analyze the subsequent moves away from free trade as follows:

> But if free trade had an obvious appeal for the industrially successful nation, it was the failure of the doctrine to deal with the problem of economic development and the complicated relations between advanced and [less advanced]

economies that formed the basis of criticism levied against it by 19th-century protectionists.[6]

Thus in the United States, for example, the McKinley act of 1890 raised the average level of tariffs to 50 percent and imposed high duties on textiles, iron, steel, glass and even on agricultural products.

The second example illustrates the important and hard-won 19th-century discovery that the values of the market must themselves be subject to higher values. Hence the prohibition of the slave trade and finally of slavery itself throughout most of the world. Similarly, Lord Shaftesbury and the early trade unionists fought long and hard against the use of child-labour in British coal mines, even though many industrialists argued that such prohibitions would surely harm those families who would no longer have the income brought home by their children.

With the expansion of trade came also the phenomenal transformations in communications and transportation: from sailing ships to steamships to airplanes, from cable telegraph to radio to television. Now, as we move into the 21st century, we are caught up in three more major shifts in the long process of globalization.

The first shift is marked by the end of the Uruguay Round and the signing of the Marrakesh agreement in April 1994 and the establishment of the World Trade Organization in 1995 to coordinate and encourage the systematic reduction of tariffs and the abolition of subsidies. It should be noted that there are in fact two kinds of trade liberalization: (1) between individual countries around the world, and (2) "bloc-based" or "power-based" liberalization, which works by consolidating a specific trading bloc such as NAFTA or the European Union.

The second major shift comes in the realm of communications: the rapid expansion of interactive, personal-computer-based information exchange, most familiar through the Internet and the World Wide Web. This seems to have caught everybody, not least the leaders of the personal computer revolution, off guard.

The third important dimension of globalization (although I shall not focus on it in this paper) is global migration, as people seek in increasing numbers to move across national boundaries.[7]

* * *

In seeking to respond to the implications of all this, we need to be clear about the perspective from which we are speaking. And within the family of the World Council of Churches, our response must be from the perspective of all those around the world who find themselves at this stage of history impoverished, powerless and excluded from the centres of wealth and power. Our concern must be with those who are most vulnerable to being manipulated or used by others.

From the perspective of Africa, and indeed of the entire developing world, four things should be said.[8]

1. There is nothing wrong with globalization per se. Clearly the abolition of the Corn Laws, with the enormous increase in trade that followed, was a good thing. It is the form or shape which globalization takes that matters. This point was made strongly by President Cardoso of Brazil in an address at the University of the Witwatersrand in Johannesburg recently. In assessing the form globalization takes in a particular context, it is critical to understand the power relations. Who is making the rules? For example, in protecting the agricultural production of its members (such as sugar beet farmers), the European Union ensures the maintenance of rules that run fundamentally counter to the whole spirit of liberalization which, the wealthy countries of the world regularly tell poorer countries, should be the norm. Would the rules of the WTO allow South Africa to encourage further wheat production by raising rather than lowering the current levels of production? Of course, any economist can produce numerous arguments why South Africa should not be so myopic as to want to do this and these arguments may indeed be convincing. Yet there could be circumstances in which, for the medium term at least, such a policy would make sense within South Africa. Indeed, for sub-Saharan Africa as a whole it is acknowledged by all that the projected impact of liberalized trade policies is likely to be negative.

2. While it is necessary to recognize that the debt crisis is a consequence of irresponsible borrowing beyond their means by governments of developing countries, it is equally fundamental to acknowledge that the debt trap in which so many poor countries now find themselves is no less a direct consequence of the irresponsibility of the powerful banks and governments which lent the money. The debt crisis in fact is itself an expression of irresponsible globalization.

The debt trap limits the accumulation of capital within those countries which need it most. It leads to the necessity of structural adjustment, which if badly managed can easily create social conflict. This can in turn depress domestic demand in a way that limits the size of the market and effectively dampens the possibility of achieving the critical mass necessary for industrial growth. Moreover, otherwise good governments become less democratic as they seek to manage the social conflict engendered by these adjustments.

3. In the first two centuries of industrialization the process of economic growth was accompanied by a steady rise in the strength of trade unions as a countervailing power to that of employers. But in the countries in the first flush of industrialization in the late 20th century this is not so. Transnational corporations, many of them with a turnover considerably greater than that of dozens of individual countries, have a power undreamed of by the earlier industrial barons, who were increasingly constrained by trade unions and the laws which workers and their supporters voted to enact. As the United Nations' *Human Development Report 1997* points out, the corporate sales of General Motors in 1994 were greater than the gross domestic products of Turkey and Denmark; the corporate sales of Nestlé were greater than the GDPs of Egypt and Nigeria.[9] It does not of course follow from this that large corporations necessarily have bad labour practices. But the fact remains that their operations, unless carefully monitored, can easily weaken trade union power – which has been necessary in all countries that have enacted effective laws to protect workers against dangerous and inhuman productive practices. Moreover, it is trade unions which have often played the leading role in mediating the impact of technological change in the patterns of production in such a way that the costs of adjustment are not borne by workers alone.

Two factors are eroding the constraints against the unchecked power of unscrupulous employers. One is the ideology of free-market, laissez-faire capitalism which accompanies much of the rhetoric of free trade. The other is the crossing of international boundaries by firms and by investors pushing capital into new ventures, in order to evade the constraints of industrial law in particular countries. In some situations – and I am not referring only to the poorer countries in the world – working conditions are as bad as anything described by Dickens. Even more devastating, perhaps, are the sudden shifts in both techniques and geographical location of production, leaving no time for the necessary adjustment of workers and communities caught up in these changes.

Marginalized groups are more vulnerable. In this phase of globalization the most exposed are electronics and clothing workers, who feel the brunt of tariff reductions leading to job insecurity and increases in home-based work. Again, not all home-based industry is necessarily bad. But without adequate monitoring, it is wide open to malpractice.

Globalization also exerts a steady pressure against widely followed policies of local preferences for state procurement. The current (albeit non-binding) protocol to make foreign companies equal to local ones in this context makes the development of local industry that much more difficult.

The mobilization of capital has massive consequences for relatively small economies, as has been seen in recent years particularly in Mexico. South Africa's own currency crisis in early 1996 faced the policy-makers of the new democratic government with the harsh realities of the pervasive power of money markets in what is increasingly a "casino world".

4. The use of poorer countries as dustbins for untouchable rubbish, such as radio-active waste, which richer countries are increasingly unwilling to keep in perpetuity in their own backyards, is a particularly unsavoury dimension of globalization – as is the practice of taking advantage of their economic weakness to produce goods there using more toxic or dangerous processes that are no longer acceptable in wealthier countries.

* * *

Let me conclude by offering a South African perspective on four dimensions of sustainable development.[10]

1. "Making development sustainable means moving beyond a narrow, albeit important, concern with economic growth *per se* to considerations related to the quality of that growth. That is, ensuring that people's basic needs are being met, that the resource base is conserved, that there is a sustainable population level, that environment and cross-sectoral concerns are integrated into decision-making processes, and that communities are empowered."

2. "Sustainable development links formerly separate discourses and asks different kinds of questions. It is the Truth Commission in the development debate."

3. "Sustainable development... requires, among other things, a massive educational effort so that citizens are made aware of the need to manage resources wisely... not only to fulfil their own needs today, but those of their children tomorrow, and of future generations. It is a concept which is in harmony with deep-seated African cultural values concerning the continuity of the dead, the living and the yet unborn."

4. Much that has been written about sustainable development concerns the natural resource base. It is important to concentrate also on human resource sustainability.

Once we focus on human resource sustainability, we are compelled to consider issues of marginalization, unemployment and the whole impact of globalization. From the perspective of those who find themselves at the sharp, painful end of globalization, how can the process can be shaped in such a way that the world of the 21st century becomes truly sustainable?

NOTES

[1] This section draws on my paper "Reflections on Work in a Sustainable Society", *The Ecumenical Review*, vol. 48, no. 3, July 1996, pp.272-78.
[2] See for example, Thomas R. Karl, Neville Nicholls and Jonathan Gregory, "The Coming Climate", *The Scientific American*, May 1997.
[3] Wilson, *op. cit.*, pp.275-76.
[4] Florence Ziumbe, "Work in a Sustainable Society: A View from Africa", unpublished preparatory document no. 6, second Visser 't Hooft memorial consultation, June 1995.
[5] "Trade Liberalization, Society and the Environment", *The Ecumenical Review*, vol. 48, no. 3, July 1996, pp.345-53.
[6] A.G. Kenwood and A.L. Lougheed, *The Growth of the International Economy 1820-1980*, London, Allen & Unwin, 1983, p.81.
[7] For an analysis of current dimensions of this problem see Myron Weiner, *The Global Migration Crisis*, New York, HarperCollins, 1995.
[8] I am especially indebted to Ebrahim Patel, deputy general secretary of the South African Clothing and Textile Workers' Union (SACTWU) for his considerable help in clarifying my thinking on these matters. Needless to say he is not responsible for what I have written here.
[9] *Human Development Report 1997*, table 4.1, p.92.
[10] Barry Munslow, Patrick FitzGerald and Anne McLennan, *Sustainable Development: Visions and Realities*, pp.3-4.

Defining Terms

EDWARD DOMMEN

This presentation will compare two concepts: *sustainable development* and *sustainability*. It is often said that the concept of sustainable development in particular has a variety of meanings, from which some commentators draw the conclusion that it is unclear, unusable or emotive. It is therefore important to be clear about the definition of both terms.

The World Commission on Environment and Development provided an official definition of "sustainable development" in its 1987 report *Our Common Future*; and this was endorsed by the UN general assembly later that year. The ecumenical movement has given a definition to "sustainability" which was included in the report of the Visser 't Hooft consultation in 1993.[1]

After examining the two definitions, we shall look briefly at the present state and limits of the consensus regarding these concepts.

Sustainable development

The formal definition of sustainable development by the Brundtland commission is as follows:

> Sustainable development is development that meets the needs of the present without compromising the ability of future generations to meet their own needs. It contains within it two key concepts:
> – the concept of "needs", in particular the essential needs of the world's poor, to which over-riding priority should be given; and
> – the idea of limitations imposed by the state of technology and social organization on the environment's ability to meet present and future needs.[2]

1. Priority to the poor

Priority to the poor according to this definition over-rides intergenerational considerations. It is the core of sustainable development.

With this demand theologians and others in the Christian tradition should feel at home. As Calvin once said, "It would be superfluous to quote many passages on the subject, since the whole scriptures are so full of them that no one can be unaware of them" (*Against the Sect of the Libertines*).

We know that this priority is due and how to achieve it, but we do not act on it. As the *Book of Common Prayer* says: "We have left undone those things which we ought to have done; and we have done those things which we ought not to have done; and there is no health in us." Our persistent failure to do the obviously needful in this case is but another manifestation of our inherent sinfulness.

It is worth stressing that the Brundtland commission's demand for "over-riding priority" to the essential needs of the world's poor is more categorical than the one used by the Roman Catholic Church, "preferential option for the poor".

2. Justice between generations

This is a more novel issue in ethics. Neither the Bible nor other expressions of religious tradition håve much to say about it.

But the careful wording of the Brundtland commission brings this novel challenge within categories which we are used to handling. The key phrase in this part of the definition of sustainable development is "to meet their own needs". In other words, we the present generation are enjoined to respect the freedom of future generations to set their own priorities rather than to have ours imposed on them. Hans Visser 't Hooft stressed this point in his contribution to the 1993 Bossey consultation, quoting John Rawls: "'All generations have their appropriate aims. They are not subordinate to one another any more than individuals are.'... Persons should be free to define anew their common values (the 'aims' of their generation) at each moment of history."[3]

The Brundtland commission renders the requirement of justice between generations operational by its insistence on *not compromising* the ability of future generations to meet their own needs. We are enjoined not to do things which actually reduce the ability of future generations to meet their own needs. To cut back on education or child health, as neo-liberalism in general and the International Monetary Fund in particular are now insisting, is contrary to sustainable development. So is nuclear waste.[4]

3. The ability of the environment to meet present and future needs

The third element of the definition is actually polemical: it was intended as an attack on the view, defended in particular by the Club of

Rome, that the world is in danger of running out of resources. The Brundtland commission takes the position that it is the state of technology and social organization which sets limits on the ability of the environment to meet the needs of humanity. It sees changes in the environment, including resource endowment, as challenges not only to humanity's inventiveness or technological prowess, but also to its forms of social organization. The social message of sustainable development comes to the forefront here again.

Sustainability

For a consultation of churches, it is surprising that, in defining sustainability, the 1993 Visser 't Hooft consultation firmly took the position which the Brundtland commission had attacked, expressing concern not for people and their freedom but for the very specific issue of the rate of consumption of physical resources:

> The consultation describes a sustainable society as one which leaves the world as rich in resources and opportunities as it inherited. This means that renewable resources are consumed no faster than they can be renewed, that non-renewable resources are consumed no more rapidly than renewable substitutes can be found, that wastes are discharged at a rate no greater than they can be processed by nature or human devices.[5]

The report continues immediately with a call for a conceptual reorientation of today's economies which is more in the spirit of sustainable development, although there are some noticeable differences:

> A *conceptual reorientation* of today's economies must take into account:
> 1) the decrease in the world's capacity to absorb the consequences of human activity in the global economy as it is currently organized;
> 2) the devastation of resources fundamental to life on earth as we know and use it, resources once considered unlimited and indestructible;
> 3) a perspective of the economy as a subset of a larger cultural and environmental whole;
> 4) a definition of "abundance" based not on growth but on sufficiency which includes values such as love and human caring;
> 5) that massive poverty and the lack of basic resources for millions are integral to the environmental problem;
> 6) the primary responsibility of industrialized countries to take immediate steps to transform their current economic systems into models which could be sustainable elsewhere.[6]

The first of these factors, which refers to the global economy *as it is currently organized*, echoes the third element of the Brundtland commission definition of sustainable development.

The second expresses a fear of the consequences of the depletion of resources for life on earth *as we know and use it*. Here is a hint of the intergenerational imperialism which the Brundtland commission so carefully avoided. Our aim should surely be to preserve the freedom of future generations to meet their own needs, not to maintain the life-style as we know it.

Indeed, the very definition of what counts as a resource is established by technology and social organization and changes from generation to generation. Oil and uranium were not resources all that long ago. On the other hand, nettles, which were considered a resource within living memory in Europe, are hardly regarded as such now. In the 19th century, there was a whole industry exporting ice from the Lac de Joux in northwestern Switzerland to Paris. The lake still freezes in the winter, but the ice is no longer an exportable resource.

The fourth remark is an essential point. The churches are on firm ground when they insist on "sufficiency which includes... love and human caring". But point 5 is disappointingly weak. Massive poverty is not just an aspect of the environmental problem; it is an insult to God. The challenge of poverty belongs at the core of our concerns, where the Brundtland commission puts it. Since social organization and technology define what count as resources, it is not so much lack of resources which is a problem, but lack of *access* to them. That, once again, is a problem of social organization.

Regarding point 6, it is sensible to act first where one has influence. It is therefore sensible for industrialized countries to take immediate steps to transform their own economic systems. But while it is true as a matter of fact that the industrialized economies serve as a model for the rest of the world, it does not follow that industrialized countries should actually strive to assert their own form of organization as a model, as (6) implies. Respect for the autonomy of future generations, which sustainable development stresses, applies equally to people of the present generation but elsewhere. The tale of the tower of Babel is a story of hope (Gen. 11:1-8).

Sustainable development in current usage

Words have a life of their own, and they evolve during their life. "Sustainable development" is no exception. It is common to truncate the definition to part of its first element. To take one recent example, a press communiqué in April 1997 announcing the Swiss federal council's "Strategy for Sustainable Development" defines it as "development that meets the needs of the present without compromising the ability of future generations to meet their own needs", citing the Brundtland commission as its source.

The "Strategy" itself does not contain the definition cited in the press release. In fact, the meaning implicitly given to the term in the document is much closer to the full Brundtland definition. Its first paragraph, referring to the transition to sustainable development in the words of the UN general assembly resolution which endorses the Brundtland report, enumerates the challenges in these fields: "social (widening gap between rich and poor, growing unemployment), economic (effects of the globalization of the world economy) and environmental".

The Swiss federal council thus accepts the conventional current view that sustainable development has three aspects: social, economic and environmental. The order of these is not standardized. It is therefore particularly welcome that the federal council not only lists the social dimension first, but mentions the gap between rich and poor as the first issue within it. Later on the "Strategy" declares the intention of the council to ask parliament to ratify the International Labour Organization conventions on trade union freedom and collective bargaining and on child labour.

Sustainable development remains a useful vehicle for furthering the social message of the gospels.

Who are the future generations?

Let us end, not with a conclusion but with food for thought. So far we have skirted an obvious question: Who are the future generations? Exodus 20:5-6 points in the direction of an answer:

> I the Lord your God am a jealous God, visiting the iniquity of the fathers upon the children unto the third and fourth generation of them that hate me; and showing mercy unto thousands of them that love me, and keep my commandments.

"Generation" has two meanings, both of which are used in this passage. Within a family it is the parents as distinct from the grandparents, children and grandchildren; for society as a whole it is the set of people alive at any one time.

Roughly speaking, three to four generations in the first sense make up the community living on earth at any one time. God "visits the iniquities" of the inhabitants of the earth on none other than themselves. On the other hand, if the human community respects God's commandments, God will show his faithfulness anew to each generation in turn, generation after generation. *That* is sustainability.

What then are God's commandments, and how does humanity show its love for God? We recalled the answer at the beginning of this presentation. If society bends all its efforts to meeting the needs of the poor first, it will generate a life-style which can be maintained indefinitely.

NOTES

[1] Cf. *Sustainable Growth: A Contradiction in Terms*, Geneva, Visser 't Hooft Endowment Fund for Ecumenical Leadership, 1993.
[2] World Commission on Environment and Development, *Our Common Future*, New York, Oxford U.P., 1987, p.43.
[3] Hans Visser 't Hooft, "Obligations to Future Generations: A Short Essay on the Ethics of Sustainability", in *Sustainable Growth*, p.97.
[4] Cf. E. Dommen, "La colonisation de l'avenir: Deux exemples énergétiques", in I. Rens and J. Jakubec, eds, *Le droit international face à l'éthique et à la politique de l'environnement*, Geneva, Georg, 1996.
[5] *Sustainable Growth*, p.9.
[6] *Ibid*.

Sustainable Development and Biotechnology

JACKIE LEACH SCULLY

Biotechnology can broadly be defined as the application of biological agents in order to alter substances and to produce goods and services for human use. Under this definition, a cow could be considered a tool of bioproduction, turning substances like grass into a product – milk – used by humans. However, the term is normally limited to things which under normal circumstances would not be produced, or which are produced on a larger scale than would occur in nature. Although "biotechnology" is a relatively recent term, many of its classical techniques are so familiar that we may not immediately think of them as technological. The skills of biotechnology go back to any ancient culture which used micro-organisms to make beer, wine or yoghurt.

Classical biotechnology exploits metabolic processes already present in living organisms, often micro-organisms (bacteria, fungi). The parallel modern development of gene technology has opened up the possibility of artificially altering the genetic information of a living thing, thus changing some of those metabolic processes in ways which make the end product more useful to humans. Classical biotechnology and gene technology are quite separate in terms of both conceptual background and the techniques they use; however, they do go hand in hand, and much of gene technology is useful only when harnessed to some kind of biotechnological process. For example, it has been possible for some years to alter bacteria genetically to enable them to make human insulin. This would be interesting but not very useful if we did not also have the biotechnology to grow these bacteria on an industrial scale to supply the diabetics of the (affluent) world.

Turning now to sustainable development, there is an evident conflict between the growth of human populations (and hence of the demands made on the environment) and the ability of the environment to meet those demands. Perhaps simplistically, one could say that solving this difficulty requires either reducing human demands (or switching them to some more sustainable form) or inducing the environment to produce more of what we need in ways which do less damage. These are in fact two sides of the same coin. The main difference between them is the degree of significance we give to what we are calling the environment – to which I will turn later. First I will introduce briefly three areas of human demand or damage in which biotechnology will, according to its advocates, come to our rescue (though its opponents say it may only make matters worse). These areas are food production (primarily agriculture), health and environmental protection.

Food

Much of the world is hungry, but there is disagreement about precisely why that is so – whether the problem lies primarily in global food production, or in global food distribution, or in both. Whatever the causes (and they are likely to be complex) in the short term the problem can only get worse: while the world's population is growing at about 2 percent a year, annual food production is growing at only 1 percent, and even that may decrease as the last benefits of the Green Revolution of the 1960s are squeezed out. Even if it is mainly the existing systems of food distribution which are at fault, changing those will clearly take large-scale political and social action: in the short term, something must be done *within* the existing systems to increase food production. What does biotechnology offer to agriculture?

By direct genetic manipulation, or by more conventional techniques assisted at some stage by genetics, biotechnology has the potential to increase the yields of food crops, increase the nutritional content of those yields, make plants resistant to diseases and pests, help in the diagnosis of plant diseases, enable plants to grow in conditions which are otherwise too hot, cold, dry, wet or salty, and produce plants that are resistant to chemical herbicides or pesticides. Many of these things are precisely what agrarian societies through the centuries have been trying to do by the more laborious methods of classical plant-breeding. Although the technology for cultivating plant cells and tissues and for combining plant cells of different species has been available for some time, it was only possible to combine this with genetic techniques from about the early 1980s; and the first field tests of crop plants modified by gene transfer (so-called transgenic plants) took place in 1986. By 1995, more than 60 plant species had been genetically engineered and over 4000 field tests of transgenic crops had taken place worldwide. The number is now much greater. Apparent successes are being reported: a "super rice", produced by the International Rice Research Institute in the Philippines, could supposedly provide an extra 100 million tons per year, and a "super cassava" gives a yield ten times greater than other strains.

What are the problems here?

The Green Revolution was at least partly responsible for increasing annual world food production by over 50 billion tons in the thirty years from 1955. On those terms, the Green Revolution was a success. But the new crop varieties which it introduced depended on increased use of fertilizers and pesticides. Many would now say that this is responsible for increasing pollution and health problems created by toxic chemicals, for fostering monoculture and reducing biodiversity, and for putting the economies of third-world countries into the hands of agrochemical multinationals. It is easy to imagine similar problems resulting from an equivalent biotechnology revolution. A major criticism of the spread of genetically modified crop species is the possibility of ecological disaster, as alien species might disturb or even destroy the ecological balance of an area. This has happened in the past when alien species introduced into a newly colonized land have established themselves and become pests. The increased danger now is the unforeseeable consequences of inserting completely new genetic combinations into an environment. This does not mean it should not be done, simply that any risk assessment in this area will necessarily be inadequate since it is, if we are honest, more a matter of imagination than hard data.

Similarly, since the major investment in agricultural biotechnology is by agrochemical concerns, the emphasis at the moment is on those developments which are most profitable for the company. For farmers, the most useful transgenic crop plants would be those resistant to pests and diseases, which currently destroy up to 40 percent of the world's crops in the field. For the world's population as a whole, the most useful transgenic crop plants might be those which are able to grow in inhospitable areas which cannot now be cultivated. Companies however are predominantly interested in developing crops linked to particular herbicides or pesticides which they can also sell. Thus, of all the transgenic crops being tested in OECD countries in 1994, the largest proportion (36 percent) were herbicide-tolerant, while only 14 percent were improvements in quality or were virus-resistant. Not only that, but the plant species used are those where potential sales are thought to justify the investment: crops like tobacco and tomatoes, rather than millet or cassava.

In other words, biotechnology does offer a realistic chance of helping to provide a level of global food production which can sustain a growing population, and is itself environmentally sustainable – but not when the direction of the technology is driven almost entirely by the short-sighted commercial interests of the rich countries.

Health

Health is a major development issue. No country can plan for any kind of just or sustainable development if much of its work-force and its health-care system are drained by disease and disability. Globalization is beginning to reinforce the intuition that no development is sustainable if it ignores the situation of most of the globe. It is also becoming clearer that an unjust development cannot be sustained for economic, ethical and spiritual reasons.

The affluent North is already familiar with biotechnological products in health care in the form of antibiotics, which are natural products biotechnologically derived from bacteria or fungi, and in the increasing amount of medication produced by bio- or gene-technological procedures. These procedures often have significant advantages over older methods, for example in price, in purity or in being closer to a human substance (this is the case for drugs like genetically manufactured insulin, growth factors and blood-clotting factors required by haemophiliacs).

Genetic techniques also offer the hope of improving diagnostic skills. This is not a trivial matter, especially for those parts of the world where an array of infectious and parasitic diseases are poorly or not at all controlled. Correct diagnosis is essential both for appropriate rapid treatment and for tracking disease accurately so that health-care services can be structured more effectively. But accurate diagnosis is often time-consuming and requires highly trained and therefore expensive staff. Diagnostic tools using monoclonal antibodies or nucleic acid probes can be more specific, faster and cheaper.

Perhaps most importantly, biotechnology holds promise for vaccine production. Many of the infectious diseases which are largely controlled in the industrialized North still wreak what has been called silent genocide in the rest of the world. These include malaria (over 100 million cases a year), tuberculosis (over a billion cases a year, with the incidence of drug-resistant cases rapidly rising) and the simple respiratory infections which kill an estimated 10 million people (mostly children) a year. Vaccines for these either do not exist or are too expensive or fragile for use in less than ideal conditions (high temperatures and high humidity). Vaccines work at the more fundamental level of prevention, not cure or palliation, and are therefore more humane and more efficient. Moreover, the establishment of a good vaccination programme can lay the foundation for the development and delivery of a whole health service, including primary care and health education.

While all this sounds very optimistic, the problem is similar to what was said earlier about food production. Like all forms of modern biotechnology, the development of new medications, vaccines and diagnostic tests requires huge investments in research; and the key players here – pharmaceutical and gene technology companies – have limited commercial interest in researching or producing products aimed at a market which may be unable to afford them. Here again the potential benefits of biotechnology will not be realized in the right places so long as the bodies doing the research and production are driven solely by market forces.

Environmental protection

The theoretical potential of using biotechnology to protect the environment from some of the demands we put on it is considerable. Ideas have included using the often quite baroque metabolic reactions of bacteria to carry out industrial processes which now require toxic chemicals or high temperatures, and using micro-organisms to provide energy from organic waste or to clean up industrial waste products which pose a long-term environmental problem. On the whole, success in these areas outside of the laboratory has so far been rather limited, although there is disagreement about whether that is because these biotechnologies are in fact less effective than was thought, or because of a lack of political or commercial will. Moreover, the better the processes for cleaning up a mess, the less motivation there is not to make the mess in the first place.

* * *

I would conclude with two points for further reflection. One is that biotechnology uses the biological processes of other species for the benefit of the human species. Furthermore, the concern for the environment in discussions of sustainable development usually comes down to ensuring that the environment remains able to provide human beings with what we require from it. What is not addressed here is how far we can go in assuming that the environment exists more or less for our benefit. We also tend to speak of the environment as if it were something around us but entirely separate from us – and of course this is not so. Increasingly, people are questioning both these assumptions, and arguing that natural resources or creation has value in and of itself which we are denying in our exploitation of it.

At this point, talking about biotechnology begins to stray into theological waters. In re-emphasizing our human connectedness with the natural world, as the environmental movement has rightly encouraged us to do – seeing creation as God's body and ourselves as part of that body – we must not naively go to the other extreme. Humans are not quite like other species; we have not lived in nature for thousands of years. What we are trying to do now – to develop a right relationship with the rest of creation – is unprecedented. I would argue that a relationship of "harmonious communion" with the rest of creation is not possible if we mean by it a complete lack of conflict. Such harmony can only be dynamic, a constant renegotiation of the relationship between humanity and the rest of the natural world.

Second, I have mentioned political issues more than once. Any technology is political because it involves power, either over other people or over nature, and necessarily tends to reinforce the power of those who already have it. Biotechnology is no exception: it separates people into those who have power and those who do not. It is clear that the power of biotechnology is presently not in the hands of those whose needs are greatest. I would not argue that technological fixes will answer all our needs; but at the moment I do not even observe a serious attempt to see whether biotechnology can provide some help for those whose needs must have priority. Yet it might be that in turning to supplying those needs, biotechnology could be beaten into the kind of ploughshares that are ultimately of greater benefit to the entire world.

REFERENCES

Bryce W. Falk and George Bruening, "Will Transgenic Crops Generate New Viruses and New Diseases?", *Science*, no. 263, 1994, pp.1395-96.
Robert M. Goodman, Holly Hauptli, Anne Crossway and Vic C. Knauf, "Gene Transfer in Crop Improvement", *Science*, no. 236, 1987, pp.48-54.
International Food Policy Research Institute Report, 1987.
Klaus M. Leising, *Gentechnik für die Dritte Welt?*, Basel, Birkhäuser, 1991.
Karen Schmidt, "Whatever Happened to the Gene Revolution?", *New Scientist*, 7 Jan. 1995, pp.21-25.
Vandana Shiva, *Monocultures of the Mind: Reflections on Biodiversity and Biotechnology*, London, Zed Books, 1993.
Robert Walgate, *Miracle or Menace? Biotechnology and the Third World*, London, Panos Institute, 1990.
M. Williamson, "Invaders, Weeds and the Risk from Genetically Manipulated Organisms", *Experientia*, vol. 49, 1993, pp.219-24.

Climate Change and Sustainable Development

JANOS PASZTOR[1]

What is climate change?

Scientific aspects

The globe is getting warmer. This has now been established – though the rate of this warming is still quite small.[2] The likely reason for this warming is the altering due to human activity of the globe's greenhouse gas (GHG) balance. More GHGs are being pumped into the atmosphere than are being absorbed by sinks, such as the oceans and the living biomass.

The source of these GHGs is human activity, mainly the combustion of fossil fuels such as coal, oil and natural gas. There are however other important GHGs, such as methane and some complex compounds such as chlorofluorocarbons, which come from agricultural and industrial activities.

The trends are on the increase. Emissions are growing, while sinks are being reduced. The net effect is further to increase the concentration of GHGs, which in turn will raise the average global temperature. As economies grow, and as others enter the global market place, more energy is bound to be required. This may be mitigated somewhat – but not fully – by increased energy efficiency.

Global warming will not be the same everywhere. The changes will be greater in the higher latitudes and lower around the equator. The impact of global warming will be climate change: local, regional and global variations in temperature, precipitation, wind, nature and length of seasons. The increased temperatures will also make the sea level rise, which will have a major effect on coastal regions, including floods and altering of local water systems.

Global warming and the resulting climate change cannot yet be seen or felt. But by the time the problem has developed so far that its effects are clearly present, humanity will have conducted a global experiment which no serious and sane scientist would ever propose as a research project!

There is still much uncertainty about how the entire climate system works. Over the past decade, however, we have learned enough to know that we must act. Uncertainty can no longer be used as a reason for inaction.

Social and developmental aspects

Climate change is about our way of life. Part of what has enabled humanity to emerge from the animal kingdom is increasing reliance on energy conversion to multiply its abilities to control nature. In a world dominated by fossil fuels, the main reasons for climate change can be found in every economic sector and in every aspect of life. Coal burned is greenhouse gas produced. Each additional person born will stake a claim on additional energy resources to be converted. If he or she is born in a highly industrialized country, that claim will in all likelihood be far higher than that of a corresponding newborn in a poor, developing country.

Consequently, climate change is not simply about limiting emissions or reducing the disappearance of sinks. It is about the very nature of social and economic development. More importantly, it is about sustainable society and sustainable development.

Coming up with technical fixes to increase the efficiency of energy conversion and thereby reduce GHG emissions is important, especially in the short and medium term. But changing our life-styles and consumption patterns and reinventing the entire fabric of economic and industrial development are *sine qua non* solutions to the long-term problem of climate change. Our theme of "sustainability and globalization" points to some of the most fundamental issues that affect how climate change will evolve. Continued materials-based economic growth, stimulated in part by ever-increasing free trade, will undoubtedly reinforce current emission trends.

As with other issues, the poor are always hurt more than the rich, because the rich have the money and the technology to shield themselves from the effects. If sea levels rise in Tokyo or Amsterdam, residents will be able to increase the height of already existing dikes to protect the population. In Bangladesh, the resulting floods will endanger millions, and there will be nobody who can help. While the analysis is oversimplified, the conclusion is important. Different people are affected differently and, more importantly, have differing possibilities, both technical and financial, to resolve the problem.

Ethical aspects

Today's high concentration of GHGs results from the combination of very recent high emissions and long-term, cumulative emissions – both from countries which are now usually categorized as the industrialized countries. Our ancestors deforested huge areas of the globe, then burned large quantities of coal. Subsequently there has been a shift to so-called cleaner fuels such as oil and gas – though from a greenhouse perspective these can only be called slightly cleaner and only in some circumstances.

While our generation cannot and should not be held responsible for the deeds of preceding generations, it would be equally inappropriate to assign farmers in China the same responsibility for reducing emissions as Canadian farmers. This ethical affirmation is at the root of an interesting scientific approach to sharing the effects of different generations. Assume that all fossil fuels will have been burned, in addition to what has already been emitted cumulatively. By averaging the emission thus produced over the total number of people living now and in the immediate future, it is possible to calculate a "fair share". Without getting into the numbers here, it can be said that citizens of the industrialized countries are now producing far above their share, while those in developing countries have a long way to go – even those at whom fingers often point, such as China or India.

The global dimension

Climate change is a global issue par excellence. GHGs are emitted throughout the globe, caused by each individual – though, as we have seen, to differing degrees. Once in the atmosphere, an emission from one source is indistinguishable from any other emission. The greenhouse gases thus emitted are spread throughout the global atmosphere, and remain there until they are absorbed by some natural or human-related means.

The global GHG concentration will rise. While the impacts will vary from region to region, they will be felt by all countries and all individuals. Given the high level of global interdependence in both the natural and socio-economic spheres, the positive or negative impacts of climate change and its secondary effects will extend to every corner of the world.

No single country – no matter how large its economy – can tackle the problem on its own, since the effects of its actions can be completely

80 *Sustainability and Globalization*

nullified by the combined non-action of the others. For example, a country, even a large and powerful one, may decide to introduce a carbon tax to discourage excess energy consumption. But if other countries do not do the same, it may price itself out of competition, since manufacturers there will be able to produce certain goods more cheaply.[3] Every country and every individual must contribute, but their actions must be agreed and coordinated at the global level. The concept "think globally – act locally" has never applied more obviously than to this issue.

Intergovernmental response

Governments are notoriously slow to respond to problems. This is especially true when they face a problem that is new and whose impacts are not yet even visible. It is even more true of a problem like climate change, where countries have radically differing views of the same problem. It is unnecessary to elaborate in detail why Saudi Arabia has a very different view on climate change from that of the island country of the Maldives. Similarly, Switzerland, Chad and Romania do not all have the same interests in this area. Yet in recent years governments, following considerable pressure from scientists and nongovernmental organizations, have begun to act on the issue of climate change.

IPCC. During the 1980s scientists were increasingly calling the attention of governments to the problem of climate change. In response, the World Meteorological Organization (WMO) and the United Nations Environment Programme (UNEP) set up the Intergovernmental Panel on Climate Change (IPCC). The IPCC is an international forum in which government-appointed and other scientists from all over the world assess the state of the world climate, and inform decision-makers on the trends and on available options to reduce the rate of climate change.

The IPCC has now made two major assessments, both mobilizing thousands of scientists worldwide, and is expected to produce additional assessments in the future. It is the most authoritative voice on the international scene about the science of climate change, the trends and possible response measures; and it provides the key scientific input into the United Nations Framework Convention on Climate Change (UNFCCC).

INC/FCCC. Towards the end of the 1980s, the IPCC started to work on the outlines of a possible convention on climate change. By early 1990, when preparations were beginning for the 1992 Earth Summit in Rio de Janeiro, governments decided that this issue was important enough to warrant the creation of a separate process, whose unique objective would be the negotiation of a treaty on climate change. Consequently, the UN general assembly set up a sub-committee: the Intergovernmental Negotiation Committee for the Negotiation of a Framework Convention on Climate Change(INC/FCCC).

The INC/FCCC worked for two years. As planned, it negotiated a convention, which was adopted in May 1992 and opened for signature at the Earth Summit – where some 150 nations signed it.

UNFCCC. With ratification by the 50th state the UNFCCC came into force on 21 March 1994. The Conference of the Parties to the UNFCCC (COP) met for the first time in Berlin in April 1995 and established standing subsidiary bodies for implementation and for scientific and technological advice, as well as ad hoc subsidiary bodies on the Berlin Mandate and on Article 13 of the convention. In January 1996 a permanent secretariat was established, which is now headquartered in Bonn, Germany.

By June 1996, 167 governments and one regional economic organization (European Union) had become parties to the convention by ratification or accession, thereby bringing participation in it to a nearly universal level.

The convention

The UNFCCC contains an objective, a number of principles, a number of commitments and a number of organizational and administrative provisions.

Two interesting principles are the concepts of "common but differentiated responsibility" and the "precautionary principle". The former implies that the developed country parties must take initial responsibility for reducing emissions. The second implies that one cannot wait until all impacts are visible and are known with full certainty before taking measures. Action has to go in parallel with more research.

The objective of the UNFCCC is clear and appropriate for a framework convention:

> The ultimate objective of this convention and any related legal instruments that the Conference of the Parties may adopt is to achieve... stabilization of greenhouse gas concentrations in the atmosphere at a level that would prevent dangerous anthropogenic interference with the climate system. Such a level should be achieved within a time-frame sufficient to allow ecosystems to adapt naturally to climate change, to ensure that food production is not threatened and to enable economic development to proceed in a sustainable manner (Article 2).

All parties commit themselves to communicating information to other parties about their emissions and what they plan to do about them in the form of regular reports called "national communications". They also commit themselves to strive generally for reduced emissions and to increase their sinks, without committing themselves to any specific goal.

Developed country parties specifically commit themselves to the aim of not going beyond their 1990 emissions by the year 2000. They also commit themselves to provide funds and technologies to developing country parties, so that these can also implement the general commitment to strive for reduced emissions.

The UNFCCC is a framework as its name implies – and it is a pretty good framework. The UNFCCC is fairly strong about the process (for example, the national communications) and about the institutions required to move the process forward (subsidiary bodies, secretariat, financial mechanism).

Governments wanted the convention to be universal – to include all nations, big and small emitters alike. While this is a very important long-term consideration, it does make it difficult for anything to happen quickly. Consequently, even the development of a "relatively simple-looking" protocol (see below) took some three years of negotiations.

An international convention is no more than what its name applies – namely a legally binding agreement between governments. Yet governments alone cannot solve the problem of climate change. A convention is only part of the solution.

Recent developments

Since its entry into force, the UNFCCC has moved forward on a number of fronts.

Institutionalization of the convention. The UNFCCC has now established itself as a force to be reckoned with. It is an intergovernmental process that draws considerable attention not only from governments, but more importantly from NGO circles and from the media. It has a financial mechanism (the Global Environmental Facility), and it has a well-functioning secretariat which cooperates with many UN and other international organizations. As it is governed by a legally binding convention which has specific commitments, it is generally expected to produce results. Since climate change is linked to practically all other aspects of sustainable development, many expect this forum to be "where the action is" in the future.

Clarification of certain issues. The convention text is unclear on many points, which were left to be resolved by further negotiations, at meetings of the Conference of the Parties or by other convention bodies. Since the entry into force of the UNFCCC, many such negotiations have taken place on a wide range of issues touching all parts of the convention. These are found as decisions of the Conference of the Parties and in the reports to their meetings. Examples include the development and implementation of a methodology for the national communications about emissions and policies mentioned above and the clarification of the status of the financial mechanism of the convention.

The Berlin Mandate. One of the most important outcomes of the first meeting of the Conference of the Parties was an agreement that the existing commitments in the convention – such as the aim of keeping the 1990 emission levels by the year 2000 – did not go far enough and that an additional protocol or other legal instrument had to be negotiated in order to bring the world closer to satisfying the objective of the convention.

In response to this so-called Berlin Mandate, the parties set up an ad hoc group to negotiate a protocol by the end of 1997 at the third meeting of the Conference of the Parties in Kyoto, Japan. The Kyoto Protocol was expected to be the first of many that will be added to the Framework.

The Kyoto Protocol. The Kyoto Protocol, adopted unanimously on the final day of the meeting in December 1997, lays down legally binding emissions targets for developed countries for the post-2000 period. Together they must reduce their combined emissions of six major greenhouse gases by at least 5 percent by the period 2008-2012, calculated as an average over these five years. Cuts in the three most important gases – carbon dioxide (CO_2), methane (CH_4) and nitrous oxide (N_2O) – will be measured against 1990 emissions. Cuts in three long-lived industrial gases – hydrofuorocarbons (HFCs), perfluorocarbons (PFCs) and sulphur hexafluoride (SF_6) – can be measured against 1990 or 1995. The protocol will come into force 90 days after it has been ratified by at least 55 countries to the convention, which must include developed countries representing a minimum of 55 percent of this group's total 1990 carbon dioxide emissions. As of 25 August 1998, 50 countries had signed the protocol.

By reducing greenhouse gas emissions to 5 percent below 1990 levels by the year 2010, the protocol will result in emissions levels that are approximately 29 percent below what they would have been in the

84 *Sustainability and Globalization*

absence of the agreement. It allows countries a certain degree of flexibility in how they make and measure their emissions reductions. In particular, a clean development mechanism will enable industrialized countries to finance emissions-reduction projects in developing countries and receive credit for doing so. An international emissions-trading regime will alow industrialized countries to buy and sell excess emissions credits amongst themselves. How these mechanisms will work will be one of the issues on the agenda of the fourth meeting of the Conference of the Parties in Buenos Aires in November 1998. The economic and political implications of the decisions and procedures adopted there will be extremely significant.

Some questions

While the negotiations continue, a number of legitimate questions are being – and indeed should be – asked. Some have no easy solutions, but by raising them one can at least advance the debate.

Can we solve the problem of climate change? The answer is a resounding yes. With a combination of technical fixes for the short and medium terms (such as increased efficiency, a shift to alternative energy supplies, improved forest management) and with the continuation of the technical fixes and progressive shifts in life-styles and consumption patterns (for example, continued economic growth with decreasing materials content, alternative human settlements planning, diminishing economic differences between North and South), it is possible to reduce emissions sufficiently to bring GHG concentrations to levels that would satisfy the objective of the convention. It will not be easy, but it is clearly feasible.

Are we moving fast enough? The answer is probably no. If one looks at the rate of climate change we are now experiencing, the projected increase in this rate and the consequent impacts, we can safely say that the response is far below what is needed. To make matters worse, initial analysis of the national communications thus far received indicate that developed countries as a whole will not even reach the relatively easy aim of keeping their emissions to 1990 levels by the year 2000.

Recognizing that developing countries need tremendous economic growth to get them out of their existing low levels of development, which itself will undoubtedly (though not necessarily) require increased emissions, one sees that we should indeed be moving much faster.

Can we move beyond technical fixes? The emphasis has been on energy efficiency, alternative energy technologies and generally doing whatever we now do but doing it better – in other words, technical fixes.

Governments, however, are not much inclined to discuss the question of life-styles, consumption patterns, or the general nature of the economic-industrial society. Yet, while in the short term technical fixes are essential, unless these longer-term issues are tackled the world will not be able to move towards full satisfaction of the objective of the UNFCCC. Governments need to be encouraged to start taking up these issues.

What about life-styles? The concept of alternative life-styles is at the centre of the debate about solutions other than technical fixes. While the world has evolved a great deal from "small is beautiful" and the various reports of the Club of Rome, the essential picture has not changed. The industrialized developed countries continue to speed along their development paths with a particular life-style (and the corresponding emissions), while the rest of the world is doing everything to try to keep up (though mostly unsuccessfully!).

The issues are complex, and usually have to do with the most fundamental aspects of how societies are set up: the relationships between home, work-place and leisure and on how one is transported from one to another; the increasing globalization through trade, breaking down certain barriers, and through the shift of power from elected officials to the ones who own the stocks; the consumer society; the increasingly materials-based economic growth. While these issues have been analyzed and debated many times over, they have not reached the agendas of the negotiators.

Should the developing countries also commit themselves to reductions? The short answer to this would seem to be "not yet" – though it must be acknowledged that different parties hold radically differing views on this. According to the "common but differentiated responsibility" principle, it is the industrialized countries that must first implement concrete policies with results before the developing countries can be expected to take up commitments themselves. As mentioned above, the developed countries have not yet convincingly shown the rest of the world that they can even reach the present aim of the convention.

At more practical levels, developing countries are waiting to see the impact of the Kyoto Protocol, which for the first time commits the developed countries to specific targets within concrete time frames. Three to five years after the entry into force of this protocol (perhaps around 2005) it should be possible to evaluate the extent to which the industrialized countries are taking this seriously. If the analysis is positive, I believe the industrialized countries will then be on sufficiently strong grounds to draw in the developing countries, and developing countries will also be ready to start assuming their responsibilities. However, there is tremendous political pressure on the developing countries from some countries, such as the USA, that they commit themselves to some form of emission reduction scheme, even if voluntary. These issues will be further negotiated in Buenos Aires.

Can we trade emissions? Some form of emissions trading is made possible by the convention. The Kyoto Protocol has gone even further. Negotiations are now under way, and it is expected that the initial results will be available by the fourth meeting of the Conference of the Parties in Buenos Aires in November 1998. However, in the longer term it would be difficult to envisage a climate change regime without some kind of trading of emissions, or emissions quotas.

A related issue is that of "joint implementation", according to which one party to the convention may reduce the emissions of another party and thereby get some credits. While the basic principle looks simple, this has proved to be one of the most contentious issues of the entire convention process. The Kyoto Protocol has taken this debate even further by introducing the concept of the clean-development mechanism. While joint implementation would be carried out by developed-country parties, the clean-development mechanism would provide for a radically new way of reducing emissions in developing countries, contributing to their sustainable development and at the same time allowing developed-country parties to earn emissions credits. Politically these are highly complicated and sensitive issues, the details of which are now being worked out by the parties.

Both "emissions trading" and "joint implementation" are ethical and political minefields. If developed countries can continue their life-styles and economic-industrial development undisturbed (since they can earn emissions credits through joint implementation by perhaps planting some forests in Africa), then the longer-term issues of climate change are not being tackled. Similarly, if through joint implementation a developed country picks up all the cheap and easy carbon-reduction projects in a developing country, then later, when that country is ready to do its share, it will have to invest much more for the same level of reduction. And what would be done with a country that went "bankrupt" after borrowing too many emission reduction credits which it cannot pay back?

The role of the churches

Governments have an important role in ensuring that the convention is implemented and that the atmosphere is protected. Non-governmental organizations (NGOs), including the churches, have an equally important part to play in this process. The convention has been set up as a rather open process, with a strong place for NGO activities; and it is to a large extent up to the NGOs to make full use of these possibilities. Let me highlight three areas in which the churches can offer an important contribution.

Clarifying ethical dimensions. The principles on which the UNFCCC is based include a number of important ethical elements. Ethical responsibility to succeeding generations is one very relevant factor. However, this is far from the only issue. As we begin to move into the post-Kyoto period of implementing the convention and its new protocol, a number of other key issues will come up requiring that previously developed ethical stances be strengthened and new ones developed. The churches will need to follow closely the decisions of the Conference of the Parties in this regard, first to identify all the relevant ethical issues, then to initiate appropriate reflection, debate and consistent action on these.

Supporting equity issues. The equity dimension of just about everything to do with climate change is very dominant. Who emits? Who pays? Who benefits? Who should pay for a carbon tax or a tax on some other natural resource? Who should change life-styles – the few high emitters or the many low emitters? Who should finance the developing world's transition to a post-fossil era? Should there be a global "Climate Plan", like the Marshall Plan in Europe after the second world war?

At a completely different scale, there have been numerous international "agreements" to increase real financial flows to the South. This has not happened, and there continues to be a need. Such transfers can include outright grants to developing countries, preferential loans, or in a more utopian context, true global taxation, and consequent resource flows. Such developments will not take place unless those who now have those resources can be convinced to do so.

Engaging the church, engaging the individuals. The churches, among many other things, are movements – movements of groups of people and individuals for the advancement of the human condition for all. Through their reflection, debate, action and example-setting, churches have already contributed – but could contribute much more – towards the implementation of the convention. Article 3 is concerned with principles, including ethical ones. Article 6 talks about public awareness. Churches have been very active in raising awareness about issues of race, gender, development and many other facets of society and development. Climate change is no exception.

Nobody is suggesting that the churches should concentrate on developing new, climate-friendly energy technologies – churches are usually not very good at things like that. However, discussion of life-styles, consumption patterns, family planning and equity issues – which to some extent are already important – will eventually shift to the centre of the climate change debate. These are areas which the churches as institutions, and as a collection of people in a movement, can and should tackle. Let us hope they will.

NOTES

[1] The views expressed in this paper are those of the author, and should not in any way be attributed to the parties of the UNFCCC. The paper has been slightly revised by the author to reflect the major developments since the time of the Bossey consultation.
[2] The presentation in this paper is deliberately qualitative. Those seeking detail about the quantitative aspects of climate change may consult the *Second Assessment Report* of the Intergovernmental Panel on Climate Change (IPCC), Geneva, 1996.
[3] It should be noted that there is some debate about the results of a carbon tax. Many believe that in the medium term such a tax may end up improving the competitiveness of a country by making processes more efficient in general.

Discerning the Causes of Globalization

DANIEL RUSH FINN

Globalization is an immensely important development for each of us, for each of our nations and for our world.[1] Of course, our planet has always been global. What is usually meant by "globalization" is the process by which our daily lives have been transformed by influences arising from distant regions of the earth.

The moral concern of Christians has rightfully been aroused by the fact that many people, especially among the world's poor, have been left worse off than before by this process. This has led many Christians to condemn globalization as a fundamentally misdirected process. The difficulties with this judgment are several, but two require comment here. The first is that globalization has not only left many people worse off, but has also left many people better off – including many of the world's poor. When poor people are made better off, they obviously become less poor and perhaps no longer poor at all. Thus the fact that globalization has helped them seems to lose its moral importance in the eyes of many, since the *poorest* apparently are not being helped. Far greater care must be taken by all our nations for the damage done to people's lives by economic change, but the benefits of that change must enter our moral assessment as well.

The second problem is that many of the effects attributed to globalization are in fact effects of other processes which would have occurred within individual nations even without increased global connectedness. Even within a single nation, the ordinary developments of economic life regularly leave some people better off and others worse off. Thus responsibly attributing economic problems to globalization requires more than a simple assertion. Quite rightful moral indignation at the plight of poor people today does not justify, however vociferous the indignation, every conceivable causal connection that might come to mind. Christians must remind themselves that a different intellectual process, one entailing the use of scientific arguments and empirical study, must be the basis for any such attributions.

Going further, some critics of globalization point out the large profits that many multinational corporations make through international trade. Many therefore attribute the basic causal force behind globalization to these corporations. From there it is often argued that if globalization has detrimental effects, then it would be a simple moral choice (though by no means a simple political process) to oppose the interests of these multinationals in an effort to reduce international trade and its detrimental effects. However, the relation between causal analysis and moral assessment is rarely so simple.

Although multinational corporations play an important role in the process of globalization, it is far more accurate to begin our causal analysis with a view of the role of technology in the developments which are shaping the world today. We will then illustrate this problem by taking a look at one particular case study: the transformation of agriculture.

The role of technology

Globalization has been made possible by changes in technology. It is now easier, quicker and cheaper to communicate with others and transport goods over long distances than it used to be. But what do we make of these technological changes? Are they good simply because they occur?

Two centuries ago Adam Smith pointed out the critical role that transportation plays in increasing national prosperity.[2] The key to economic growth, he observed, is "the division of labour", the specialization of workers that enables a rural family specializing in farming to produce more per year than a family that must also make its own clothes and soap and other non-farm necessities as well. As transportation improves, more specialization can occur because the same producer can serve a larger market. Economists today tend to look at international transport of goods in the same way. Larger physical markets allow for even greater efficiencies and thus increased prosperity.

However, this technical capacity to transport goods over greater distances causes disruptions, even pain in the lives of many working people. Should we thus turn to government to place limits in view of the dislocations caused? Or should we allow all such technological changes to occur simply because they are possible?

One need not be a Marxist to recognize the truth underlying Karl Marx's materialist interpretation of history. For our purposes, we can think of this insight as having two parts. The first is that when technological change occurs, it has far-reaching influence on humans and their social institutions. The second is that technological change itself appears as an independent force in our common life because it seems to be inevitable: it is extremely rare that an improvement in a production process, once discovered, is not implemented. While Marx extended the impact of such changes in the forces of production into the realm of ideas to an extent many find historically inaccurate, those two initial insights are quite relevant to the debate over globalization.

The far-reaching influence of technological change on humans and their social institutions would seem undeniable. While we today would probably think immediately of the tremendous impact of the invention of the computer in this connection, revolutionary change produced by technological developments is not a new phenomenon. Earlier the invention of the automobile transformed our cities, just as the widespread use of the tractor transformed agriculture after the first world war, just as the development of the railroad transformed entire economies in the 19th century. Historians of culture remind us that even earlier transformations, though less frequent, had similarly pervasive effects. The invention of iron and bronze now mark off whole epics of human history.

The fact is that each of these technological changes, from the computer to the use of iron, appeared as an independent "force" in the human community, whose implementation and widespread use seemed virtually inevitable once it was discovered, can be considered as threatening to a quite understandable goal of all who live within a democracy: that we as a community should be able to control our own economic and cultural development so that our fundamental values are respected. This threat of inevitability is the core of the hard message which the materialist interpretation of history has for Christian theology and ethics. Knowing that not everything which is both possible and profitable ought to be done, we are left with a critically important question: Of all the things in our world that are occurring because of technological change, which ought we to oppose directly on grounds of Christian theology and ethics? To focus more precisely on our theme: Should we restrict by law the ongoing globalization that modern transportation and communication technologies make possible?

Globalization by itself is such a massive process that it will be helpful to focus on a subset of the problems it entails. There are many we might look at, such as damage to the environment or the loss of jobs, concerning which there are widely clashing assertions about both causal and moral analysis which need careful attention. Here I shall look at another issue, the transformation of agriculture and loss of the small-scale farmer – or, as it is described in the USA, the disappearance of the "family farm".

The transformation of agriculture: a case study

The most fundamental damage caused by the transformation of agriculture over the past century and a half has been the loss of community. Farmers around the world have been moving to the city and leaving the rural areas where, were it not for economic pressures, they would have preferred to stay. The effect has been that, especially in industrialized countries, a myriad of tiny communities have shrivelled and many have disappeared completely. Many urban residents today are unsure of their own physical security and relate throughout the day to a long list of anonymous clerks, attendants and voices on the phone. In contrast, the shared family histories and pervasive mutual familiarity typical of small rural communities stand as vital though endangered reminders of the loss of community in much of modern urban life. To be sure, those rural communities have traditionally had their shortcomings: provincialism, resistance to outsiders and to diversity among their own members, a tendency to subordinate the life prospects of women to those of men. Still, their disappearance is, on balance, a great loss from the perspective of Christian faith.

At a preliminary level of analysis, there is widespread agreement that the immediate causes of this transformation of rural life have been the appearance of larger and larger farms and the ability of consumers to purchase food grown at great distances, even from nations on the other side of the globe. But if we ask what deeper causes have brought about these effects, we find immense differences of opinion. Most of those who oppose globalization, whether in agriculture or elsewhere, point to multinational firms and governments as the primary force in this process. For example, Herman Daly and John Cobb have argued that the self-interest of large agribusiness grain companies and the errors of governmental policies encouraging large-scale "industrial" farming have brought about the demise of small farms.[3] We witness a strong reaction against the transformation of agriculture in almost every industrialized country. From France to Canada to the US to Japan, farmers regularly look to national governments for financial support to allow traditional agricultural methods and rural communities to continue.

This process is related to globalization because any nation can today import food from abroad, often at lower prices than domestic farmers can offer. What prevents increased international trade in agricultural products are primarily governmental decisions in the industrialized world to create barriers to imports and to raise domestic food prices, subsidizing domestic farmers to protect them from the threat of lower prices available from other nations. To take one example, both Switzerland and the US state of Minnesota produce sugar from sugar beets, even though their relatively chilly climates are far less suited to sugar production than those of the major sugar-cane producing nations, which can depend on an abundance of warmth from nature's sunshine. If international trade in sugar were allowed without restriction or government subsidy, consumers in both the United States and Switzerland would be buying sugar from Brazil or Thailand or Cuba for a lower price than they now pay.

If one identifies only corporate greed and misplaced government policies as the causal forces in the transformation of agriculture within this globalization process, national decisions to slow or stop the process seem quite reasonable. But this approach misidentifies the causal situation. Two powerful economic forces at work in agriculture are widely misunderstood or ignored in this debate.

The first of these forces is technological change. A series of inventions over the past 200 years has transformed agriculture: the cast-iron plough, the steel plough, the grain drill, the threshing machine, the mowing machine, the revolving disk harrow, the use of electricity to light barns and pump water and chill milk, the development of the internal combustion engine that made the tractor possible, and a myriad of changes in the quality of seeds and chemicals.

A number of these changes have had important negative side effects, some of which have not yet been thoroughly addressed, including pollution caused by agricultural runoff and the depletion of aquifers. Nevertheless, there have been two predominant positive effects: a sharp increase in production per acre and, even more important, a tremendous increase in production per hour of labour time.

While the size of farms has indeed increased, the main reason for this is not corporate take-overs (in the US and Canada, less than one-half of 1 percent of all farms are owned by corporations).[4] The vast majority of small farms that are "disappearing" are simply being bought up by a neighbouring family ready to farm more acres than before. The basic fact of technological change in agriculture is that farmers themselves are choosing to alter their production methods. Though appreciating the advantages of rural life, farm families have also valued most of the amenities that a higher standard of living earlier brought to their urban counterparts. Thus, with the availability of more education, better seed varieties, labour-saving farm machinery and a host of other developments, most farmers, generation after generation, have chosen higher-skilled, higher-technology methods to increase their productivity and their incomes.

The second great force in this transformation of agriculture is a thoroughly social influence, arising from the pattern of choices people make in spending their resources. Economists refer to this as the "income elasticity" of demand for food. Consider what happens to a typical urban family whose annual income increases by 10 percent. Having more money to spend, they will tend to spend more on most things they are already purchasing. However, common sense, confirmed by empirical study, indicates that they will not spend exactly 10 percent more on everything they are currently buying. They will probably increase their expenditures on things we would call luxuries by more than 10 percent and on what would be called necessities by less than 10 percent. Simply because we become more wealthy does not mean we will use much more salt or bread than before.

In impoverished regions, where food is still a kind of luxury, people tend to spend at least 10 percent more on food when their income rises by 10 percent. In the industrialized nations, however, research has shown that when people's income rises 10 percent their expenditures on food products from the farm increase by much less than 10 percent. They may spend more on groceries and buy more meals at restaurants (on the average, people in the US spend 14 percent more on restaurants when their income rises 10 percent), but most of that money goes to food processors and restaurants, who are selling convenience. Very little increase in consumption of farm products is entailed.

In fact this has happened in all industrialized countries. As the general income of the nation rises, the proportion spent on food products falls, not because people eat less food, but because expenditures on food rise only a small amount compared to dramatic rises in spending on many other goods. This trend has been evident over the last 200 years: as national income rises, the proportion of it that goes to farm products has fallen to the point where in many industrialized countries it is now below 3 percent. Quite obviously, poorer nations spend a larger percentage of their national income on agriculture than do wealthy ones.

What then is the impact of these two forces on agriculture? The first – technological change – allows a typical farmer to till more acres and produce more products per hour than ever before. But larger farms mean there is now room for fewer farmers in a region than there was a generation ago. The second force means that while urban incomes are rising, farmers have to split up a shrinking portion of the national income and their incomes lag behind those of their fellow citizens in the cities. The incomes of farmers are nevertheless able to rise because, with technological change, farmers have become more productive. It is an unwelcome side effect of this historical process that many people will no longer have jobs in agriculture and must find other employment. Even more difficult from the point of view of Christian ethics is the loss of the vibrant sense of community which existed in rural communities, many of which have now disappeared.

It was out of a concern for the fate of the small family farm that agricultural support programmes in the industrialized nations began. The most prevalent rationale for national governments' support for agriculture is that the vagaries of weather and the fluctuation of world agricultural prices have caused intolerable problems for farmers. Every business has its risks, but farming has more than most. Cheaper transportation means that almost any agricultural product produced almost anywhere in the world can be delivered to any other point in the world without much increase in its price. A good price available somewhere else will greatly affect local farmers' ability to sell their produce. Given the fluctuations of weather and the other variables in the farm system, it is quite possible for farmers who experience two or three consecutive bad years actually to lose their livelihood altogether in the face of even temporarily low prices available elsewhere in the world. Government subsidies have used a variety of schemes to guarantee a "floor" price to farmers even when the world price for their product is permanently below this level. For those interested in saving the family farm, these support programmes appear very attractive.

On the other hand, a Christian ethical analysis of this process raises important questions. While European farmers fear the import of agricultural products from the United States and Canada (and vice versa), the system of reciprocal supports and barriers to imports in the industrialized world leaves most of these countries about equally protected from international competition while leaving completely unprotected farmers of the developing world who could otherwise sell more of their products to them.

To understand this, it is important to realize a critical anomaly in the relationships between national governments and their agricultural sectors. Although nearly all industrialized nations subsidize the farm sector, most developing nations actually penalize their farmers.[5] There are a number of reasons for this. Many developing nations want a "cheap food policy" to improve the standard of living of urban people. Even in nations where the majority lives in rural areas, governments are often most responsive to the better-educated, politically active urban classes. In some countries, national policy deliberately penalizes agriculture in an attempt to promote a manufacturing sector.

There is no doubt that the plight of the poor in the developing world could be more directly improved by a wide variety of economic policies undertaken within their own nations. Nevertheless, if the industrialized countries removed their support of domestic agriculture, farmers in the developing world would have more markets and would be better off for it.

The picture of efforts to preserve the family farm and rural communities in the industrialized world is thus a complicated one. If these historical transformations were exclusively caused by the greed of multinational firms and the misguided hopes behind national agricultural policies, Christians might understandably object to the loss of vibrant community and work hard to counteract such forces. In fact, this is the view endorsed by many people in the industrialized world who oppose greater international trade in agricultural products. If however, as has been argued here, the primary forces behind the transformation of modern agriculture have been decisions by farmers (to improve their own productivity and well-being) and by consumers (to spend most additional income on non-farm products), then an ethical analysis of the transformation of rural life must take into consideration the moral standing of these decision-makers.

There is no doubt that national governments must work to correct the problems larger farming operations have caused, including pollution and unsustainable depletion of water resources. Large-scale operations should not gain an advantage over smaller ones through irresponsible practices. However, once such adjustments are made, larger-scale farming is quite likely to remain more efficient than small-scale farming in many areas; and the attempt to thwart this long-term process by import restrictions and farm subsidies entails severe problems. Because most subsidies go to all farmers and not simply to those "needy" smaller farmers, the system is a very inefficient one. Some estimates are that as much as $11 goes to prosperous farmers in the US and Canada for every $1 that goes to a needy farmer. Second, the effort to raise farm prices in order to help farmers also raises food prices for poor people in the cities of the industrialized world. At a time when governments are cutting back on social support for the poor, this explicit policy of raising farm prices must be re-examined. Third, the well-being of rural people in the third world (both rich and poor, of course) would be improved if the industrialized countries purchased more farm products from abroad.

This very brief enquiry into modern agriculture suggests that the ethical debate over economic life must attend more carefully to causal analysis. This same principle applies to debates over the loss of jobs and environmental damage, which many have attributed too simply to international trade. Just as in the case of agriculture, international trade contributes to these problems, but it is a relatively minor causal force. As a result, railing against globalization because of these problems is largely misplaced; and hopes to solve these problems by curtailing international trade are doomed to failure.

Concluding reflections

This brief presentation has not referred to the absolutely essential enquiry into Christian theology and ethics in addressing globalization. Nor has it dealt with the important concrete steps our nations must take to mitigate the painful effects of economic adjustments caused by globalization. These are similar in kind, however, to the efforts we must make to reduce the damage caused by a variety of economic changes in each of our nations. Both normative and empirical issues need to be addressed here. However, it is discouraging that so many nations seem to be moving away from a sense of responsibility for the damage our economic systems cause in the lives of the most vulnerable. What is at stake here is the moral character of markets more generally, not whether they are limited within national boundaries. The key assertion made here is that morally concerned Christians must be very careful when assertions of causes are assumed and then integrated into a moral analysis.

I would conclude with a final note about the moral importance of the globalization process. Although there are undoubtedly negative effects, the greater awareness of and knowledge about peoples and cultures different from our own is most likely to have morally beneficial effects in the long run. We are, in the end, all children of the same God. Thus, for both religious and practical political reasons, it is dangerous for Christians to assert national sovereignty as a defence against a host of economic problems that only appear to be caused by international trade. We are in serious need of strengthening our international institutions to deal with a variety of issues from arms reduction to the environment to child labour to the rights of women.

Globalization will continue to have both good and bad effects, but neither are likely to be as large as the strident participants to the debate thus far would have us believe. Neither our hopes nor our fears for the future spring from so recent a development in world history. While globalization has its effects, our common economic future will be a just and sustainable one only if we can solve problems of which we have been long aware.

NOTES

[1] I have adapted portions of this text from my book *Just Trading: On the Ethics and Economics of International Trade*, Nashville, Abingdon, 1996. Used by permission.

[2] Adam Smith, *An Inquiry into the Nature and Causes of Wealth of Nations*, London, W. Strahan & T. Cadell, 1776; repr., ed. Edwin Cannan, New York, Modern Library, 1937, p.17.

[3] See Herman E. Daly and John B. Cobb, Jr, *For the Common Good: Redirecting the Economy toward Community, the Environment and a Sustainable Future*, Boston, Beacon, 1989, p.272.

[4] Statistics Canada, *Canada Year Book 1990*, Ottawa, Communications Division, 1989, charts 9.30 and 9.31; and US Bureau of the Census, *Statistical Abstract of the United States: 1991*, Washington, DC, p.647.

[5] See Rod Tyers and Kym Anderson, *Disarray in World Food Markets: A Quantitative Assessment*, Cambridge and New York, Cambridge U.P., 1992, ch. 2; and W.L. Peterson, "International Farm Prices and the Social Cost of Cheap Food Policies", *American Journal of Agricultural Economics*, vol. 61, no. 1, Feb. 1979, pp.12-21.

Globalization: Blessing or Curse? Buzz-word or Swear-word?

PETER TULLOCH

Economists are inclined and trained to be analytical and sceptical, particularly of jargon and ill-defined concepts. Maybe this is why I am allergic to broad, sweeping notions such as "globalization", however fashionable the word may have become.

Like most human endeavours, economics is subject to major changes in thinking – one might almost call them swings of fashion. For example, when I began as a trade economist, development theorists were moving from "import substitution" to "export orientation". Developed markets were seen as too closed to products from the developing world. The Generalized System of Preferences was at that time the favoured tool to change the situation: developed markets were to give free access for goods – particularly manufactured goods – from developing countries, in order to pull them out of their dependency on limited sources of income from commodities. The process, however, was to be one-sided: developing countries would continue to benefit from "infant industry" or "infant economy" protection through barriers to trade and foreign investment, behind which they could build up their domestic production structure.

For about twenty years this model of development continued to fascinate politicians, economists and international "experts". During the early to mid-1980s, the tide changed. Two opposing strands of thought emerged. On the one hand were the "limits to growth" theories, stemming from the realization that most resources are limited, which led to the concept of sustainable development. On the other hand was a more favourable attitude to market opening in the developing economies, stemming from a realization that the infant industry model also had its limits – limits of capitalization, limits of policy-making capacity and limits caused by rigidities associated with excessive state controls.

The flaws in the model of export-led development coupled with strict domestic protection became clear. Barriers to imports did not usually lead to production of necessities for the people but to high-cost manufacturing of goods which often imitated, less well, items produced in the developed world (although some countries, behind import barriers and with strong government guidance, did succeed in developing good, competitive products and services). At the same time, high taxation on many consumer items often led to smuggling of foreign goods by the rich for the rich. Devious ways, including the redesigning of import regulations, were found to allow the wealthy, who could travel abroad, to bring in luxury goods, while lower-income consumers were denied access to low-cost imports. In many cases the over-emphasis on export promotion led to little integration between the external sector and the domestic economy. Export goods were often produced in foreign trade zones, using imported inputs with few links to domestic inputs and little use of home-produced materials. This pattern still persists in certain Central American countries, the Philippines and Mauritius. The problem of how to promote quality industrial and agricultural development, without the leaven that foreign investment and experience could provide, became acute.

The mid- to late 1980s and the first half of the 1990s thus became a period when many developing countries, often with a push from institutions such as the World Bank, unilaterally opened up their markets to imports from developed and other developing countries. Having reassessed the value to themselves of foreign investment, they moved away from relative isolationism to greater integration into the world economy. In broad economic terms, the initial results were startling: markedly higher growth rates in developing countries which opened their markets – particularly in Asia, but also in those countries of Latin America which have managed to avoid financial catastrophes – as well as new structures of production with greater international linkages; more rapid technical change, and a shift of the economic weight in the world from Europe and North America to the Pacific Rim. The trade liberalization elements of these changes were confirmed in the Uruguay Round and the creation of the World Trade Organization.

All these factors, combined with increases in speed and scope of communications, have contributed to the process that is called globalization. Depending on the angle from which one approaches it, globalization is seen either as a blessing or a curse, as a buzz-word or a swearword. Some welcome it as a path to new patterns of growth and development; others use it as a synonym for unwelcome, over-rapid change and loss of control of the economic and social environment.

Globalization: Blessing or Curse? Buzz-word or Swear-word? 101

In whatever way one looks at it, the process being described seems irreversible. We must therefore demystify the word "globalization" by analyzing the process and seeing how it can be used constructively.

Various definitions have been offered of globalization:
– "the growing economic interdependence of countries worldwide through the increasing volume and variety of cross-border transactions in goods and services and of international capital flows, and also through the more rapid and widespread diffusion of technology";[1]
– "the widening of the spectrum of goods and services entering international trade (as) a consequence of trade liberalization, increased freedom of establishment and technical innovations allowing long-distance delivery of services";[2]
– "a process whereby producers and investors increasingly behave as if the world economy consisted of a single market and production area with regional or national subsectors, rather than of a set of national economies linked by trade and investment flows";[3]
– "the absorption of all countries and systems into one".[4]

What are the main features of the globalization process?
– an immense *increase in the volume of goods and services traded internationally*, associated with the steady and continuing process of trade liberalization; during the period from 1985 to 1995, the volume of world merchandise exports consistently grew more rapidly than world output, with average annual rates of 6 percent and 1.5 percent respectively in 1990 to 1995. Consequently, trade came to have a much greater influence on the economies of most countries;
– an equally important *shift in the country and product structure of international trade*; between 1985 and 1995, developing countries raised their share of trade from 23 to 29 percent, increased their share of trade among themselves from 31 to 37 percent, and increased the share of manufactures in their exports from 47 percent to a staggering 83 percent;
– an even larger *increase in the volume, speed and complexity of financial and direct investment flows* and a multiplication of financial markets, again involving greater integration of developing countries; private capital inflows to developing countries rose from an average of one-half of one percent of their GDP in the period from 1983 to 1989, to between 2 and 4 percent from 1994 to 1996, with the share of bank lending falling and that of direct investment rising;

- *continuing economic growth in some developing countries* at a speed never seen before in the post-second world war period; in some cases this was helped by well-directed state intervention, and in other cases by the *withdrawal* of the state from economic intervention;
- concomitant *changes in patterns of production of goods and services*; this is seen partly in an increasing shift away from manufacturing to services in Western economies, while manufacturing rises in developing countries, and partly in the fragmentation of production processes previously undertaken in one place (television sets assembled in France from parts produced in Singapore, Germany, the Philippines and Spain; computer reservation systems for British Airways or Swissair flights operated by programmers and engineers working in Bombay or Pune).

Some of the elements which have contributed to the globalization process are:
- trade liberalization, first in goods then in services, and the clear evidence that nations taking an active part in the process of liberalization have, in macro-economic terms, advanced (at least at the macroeconomic level) more rapidly than those that have not;
- freer movement of capital than of labour and freer movement of skilled labour than of unskilled labour, including the development of new skills in an educated workforce (computer programming, engineering, finance) – a trend which cuts across boundaries between "developed" and "developing" countries;
- transfer and adaptation of technologies (new agricultural methods under the Green Revolution and its successors; the application of computer technology to a whole variety of processes);
- more rapid, widespread and affordable communications (travel, telecoms, satellite TV, Internet);
- acceptance of English as the principal language of business, communication, science and education (100 years ago it was French).

The process which has grown into "globalization" has, I believe, benefited humankind in many ways. Taken together with education and other elements of social and economic development, trade and economic liberalization have lifted many people out of the subsistence economy into participation in economic development, even at a time when the population of the world is still growing very fast. For example, Kenya has had thirty years of over 3 percent population growth; yet there is evidence that the country can still feed itself and that there is a growing African middle class. The academic discussions of 30 years ago about whether India could feed its rapidly increasing population have also been belied by events: the growth rate of India's population has declined and access to food has improved.

Like any transformation, the process of globalization has not been achieved without costs, and fears about its effects are understandable. The past twenty years or so have seen an industrial revolution comparable to that brought about in the age of steam. The faster pace of change leads to greater feelings of insecurity; the real "adjustment" – too mild a term for what is often dramatic social and communal disruption – can be hard to bear.

- In many developed economies, unemployment has increased and real wages have fallen, even though the worst fears of "de-industrialization" stemming from the combination of trade, capital movements and technology have not been realized. Some countries and communities have managed to surmount the changes more or less successfully; thus, some watchmaking towns in Switzerland have been converted into centres of precision engineering; in the French Jura, historically a depressed zone, the optical industry has grown; there is now some evidence that average incomes in the United States are growing and the fear of proliferation of "McJobs" is becoming stilled. But there are still many uncertainties and feelings of powerlessness.
- Development has also been uneven in the "developing" world. Although statistics show a general increase in economic welfare, relative income distribution has worsened in many cases.
- In all economies the balance between skilled/educated and unskilled/uneducated people has increasingly tilted in favour of the more educated and hence more flexible. This leaves less skilled or less educated people and populations more vulnerable and marginalized.
- There is a general impression that the autonomy of governments in policy-making has declined. "The market" is seen as too powerful and potentially destabilizing and there is a feeling that "business has become the most powerful force shaping the world".[5] At the same time, however, markets are what we all rely on.

Political developments, sometimes linked to systemic economic change, have been equally dramatic:
- The major painful and destabilizing political transformations in Russia and Eastern Europe have not yet been consolidated.
- Equally strong economic reforms have taken place in China, leading

to double-digit economic growth (if the data can be believed) but within a very controlled political system.
- In the absence of countervailing power in Europe or elsewhere, there has been an increase in the geopolitical and educational influence of the United States, now "the only superpower".
- A new series of relationships are being created among what were formerly regarded as "East and West" and "North and South".

In the former GATT and now in the WTO, this change in international relationships has been visible both in the much greater integration and influence of the nations of the South in the work of the organization, and in changing alliances among nations in trade negotiations – for example, the creation of the so-called Cairns Group of agricultural exporting countries, which crosses the boundaries of both "North-South" and "East-West" interests in trying to combat the protectionism of the US, the European Union and Japan. Fundamental new alliances are also being forged in Latin America, Asia, Africa and Europe. In Latin America, the drive for regional cooperation (and for new ways of dealing with relations with the United States) is strengthening. In the Asia-Pacific region, ASEAN (which has expanded to ten members) and the APEC group, which takes in the whole of the Pacific basin, are becoming important cross-cultural groupings which transcend old models. The expansion of the influence of the European Union to Central and Eastern Europe and the Baltic states is filling the vacuum left by the downfall of the Soviet system. The political transformation in South Africa has raised hopes that it may be a positive and dynamic economic and political force in southern Africa if not the whole of the continent.

These changes are the new framework for the interaction between economics and politics. They are the most fundamental since the fall of European empires and the post-war reorganization, and the realities within which we and our children's generation will have to live. How should we, as social individuals and as Christians, cope with these developments? I believe we must begin by recognizing a few things.

We must recognize that rapid change often means severe adjustment and disruption; therefore, we should encourage and promote policies that do not deny change, but seek to minimize or compensate for its disruptive effects, while looking out for new opportunities to bring about positive change.

We should also recognize that markets, if undistorted, generally do operate efficiently and to the benefit of consumers. Most efforts to protect special interest groups (such as Alsatian coal-miners or US textile workers) have not worked and may in the long run do more harm than good to the people they seek to protect. The US textile industry used the 30 years of protection available under the Multi-Fibre Arrangement to restructure itself on a more capital-intensive basis. This increased profits but dramatically cut employment and distorted world textile and clothing markets in the process.

We should recognize that effective competition is essential to the good functioning of markets, and that monopolies, which necessarily distort, should be discouraged. It is evident that the privatization of British water companies on a monopoly basis has not benefited consumers, while the privatization of telecommunications on a competitive basis has done so.

We should recognize that while trade liberalization is in broad terms desirable, it is not a sufficient condition for economic growth and, in turn, that economic growth is not a sufficient condition for social development or improved income distribution.

We should recognize that market solutions can also be found to ecological concerns (responsible forestry, aided by competitive prices, can help to husband resources; exploitative mining will wear them out). The problem economists have to face is to calculate the costs appropriately. It is well recognized that GDP is far from a perfect measure; but so far a more convenient measure has not been found.

We must recognize that exploitation does exist and should be countered (for example, through internationally applied, well-monitored child labour codes).

We must recognize that there is need for active policies by governments to ensure both that markets function and that exploitation is minimized and the pain of adjustment alleviated. But we cannot deny that change is part of our lives. We must also recognize that relatively few governments meet the criterion of being "of the people, by the people, for the people".

At the national and international levels, we must recognize that rules must be designed and applied to help nations and groups to grow and develop in order to even out the differences among them. But this is not easy, given the political imbalances that exist in the world. That is part of the task which agencies like the WTO and UNCTAD are intended to face.

There has never been a golden age. Some people look back nostalgically to the Victorian era; but while it was all right if you were rich, one should read Charles Dickens or Victor Hugo. In the same way, the quest for an ideal without some kind of road map can lead to bitter disappointment. The Christian question, "Who is my neighbour?", can link economics, politics and ethics, and may help us in our thinking about "globalization" and "sustainability".

In this process, economics can be a valuable analytical tool. Economics is the science of deciding how best to use and husband scarce resources – in Christian terms, of wise stewardship. As such, it can and should be entirely consistent both with "sustainability" and with Christian ethics. The problem to be addressed is how we as fallible human beings and Christians are to apply these disciplines in a "globalized" world.

NOTES

[1] International Monetary Fund, "Globalization: Opportunities and Challenges", in *World Economic Outlook*, May 1997.
[2] Ronald W. Jones and Henryk Kierzkowski, "Globalization and the Consequences of International Fragmentation", unpublished paper, Geneva, Graduate Institute of International Studies, Feb. 1997, mimeo.
[3] *Globalization and Liberalization*, New York and Geneva, UNCTAD, 1996.
[4] Rob van Drimmelen, *Faith in a Global Economy: A Primer for Christians*, Geneva, WCC, 1998, p.8.
[5] Jeffrey Garten, *The Financial Times*, 21 May 1997.

Globalization and Sustainable Prosperity

HERBERT OBERHÄNSLI

The idea of "globalization" includes two dimensions: worldwide and comprehensive. It is characterized by ever-closer linkages and by the extension of competition into more areas than before. This means, for instance, that for emerging markets, international dependence is replaced by competition, which offers them enormous opportunities.

Impact on prosperity

Overall, there have been enormous gains in prosperity worldwide thanks to globalization.

In many richer economies, structural adjustment triggered by globalization has added to an already high rate of unemployment. At the same time, however, overall gains in well-being are unprecedented in history. Within the last ten years, according to UN Development Programme statistics, 500 to 600 million people have been newly established above the poverty line. According to UNDP forecasts, the group of people living on revenues above the poverty line is expected to increase further by 1.5 to 2 billion in the 30 years to come. It is true that 600 to 700 million people may remain below the poverty line in the next 30 years, because the market mechanism will not be able to solve all problems by then. But the impact of globalization is clearly working in the right direction.

Along with higher incomes for billions of people, more and better jobs and a rapidly increasing middle class in emerging economies, a wider choice of goods and services is being produced more efficiently. It is consumers all over the world who must be seen as the main winners in this process – and not the firms (due to increased competition).

The outlook, based on World Bank data, suggests that, according to the regional pattern of future gains from globalization, even Africa will gain from globalization over the next 15 years.

108 Sustainability and Globalization

PROJECTED ANNUAL GROWTH IN PER CAPITA GROSS DOMESTIC
PRODUCT 1994-2010

Two World Bank scenarios

	"divergent" scenario	"globalization" scenario	difference between the two scenarios
	percentage of growth per annum	percentage of growth per annum	additional wealth accumulated
OECD countries	1.6	2.3	+12 percent
East Asia	3.0	4.4	+24 percent
China	2.3	3.9	+28 percent
South Asia	2.4	4.0	+28 percent
Latin America	1.4	3.3	+35 percent
North Africa/ Middle East	1.4	3.4	+37 percent
Sub-Saharan Africa	–0,3	1.7	+37 percent

Source: *IBRD World Development Report 1995*

There are a number of parallel developments – partly distinct from globalization, partly overlapping with it, partly stimulated by it, and partly accelerating it – which may be mentioned. One is the expansion of technology in general, and in particular information technology. There is also the process of de-industrialization and the growth of the service sector. The global knowledge base has increased, with a doubling of the scientific literature every 10 to 15 years. One aspect of the slow-down in population growth is the increase in learning, made possible in part because parents have more time and resources to invest in their children. It is learning which makes knowledge out of the mass of information. In many countries of the developing world there is autonomous opening, deregulation, modernization and globalization of rules and institutions relevant to business. Company behaviour is also changing, seen for example in the outsourcing to India of software development.

Prosperity in industrialized countries

There has been a slow-down in economic growth in industrialized countries. But any conclusion drawn from these statistics should take into account the error in inflation measures, improvements in health care (which does not just involve higher prices of the health-care system) and the impact of the ageing of the population.

The correction of wage compression should also be noted. Low wages act as a starting point for people joining the labour market in the United States; and 95 percent of those identified as belonging to the lowest quintile of income distribution in 1975 are no longer in that group. In Europe, the phenomenon of high minimum wages acts as a means to keep newcomers out of the job market.

In industrialized countries today, income differentiation runs along the lines of education and skills, and no longer according to entitlements, or because someone comes from a middle-class family. It should be noted that the widely publicized and very high incomes of some sports stars and corporate managers are in fact statistically not significant.

Several other factors increase the spread between high and low household incomes: the growth in the number of two-career couples, of one-person households (expected to increase from 21 percent to 30 percent in the next ten years) and of single-parent families, both in the US and in Europe.

As with inflation and growth figures, there are also matters of perception and statistical error involved here. In the UK, for instance, this can be shown from data on consumption by income class. In the bottom tenth of population according to income, statistically measured revenues decreased by 18 percent, while actual consumption increased by 14 percent. Among the reasons for this are the "shadow economy" and the changing population in this tenth.

Freedom and other values

Globalization will be sustainable only if it does not have a systematically negative impact on values and on people's attitudes.

Changes in values are taking place for many reasons other than globalization – note the statistics above on one-person households, which point to the increasing problems for stability of families.

The global challenge leads to a new selection and recombination, but not automatically to a negative selection of values. Some of the very positive aspects of this selection lead in the direction of greater freedom.

Another phenomenon to be noted is trust as a competitive advantage. According to Francis Fukuyama, "trust" refers to the propensity of people in a society to cooperate with each other and to avoid inefficient non-cooperative traps. When trust dominates, people expect certain fair or cooperative behaviour of their opponents, even those whom they do not expect to encounter again. Fukuyama argues that high trust among citizens leads to superior performance by all institutions in a society, including firms. This implies that trust is most needed – and therefore increasingly a factor of competitiveness – where there are large organizations and a global economy, in which people interact with each other infrequently. One long-term outcome of global competition is thus the growing importance of trust, because it is a recipe for success.

Trust does not develop in a short time. It is a habit formed during a centuries-long history of horizontal networks of association between people, covering both commercial and civic activities. The formation of trust is subject to certain basic conditions. For example, studies have shown that trust is lower in countries with dominant hierarchical religions. The imposition of an hierarchical structure on the society, often in symbiosis with the state, seems to discourage the formation of trust among the citizens.

In connection with the discussion of globalization and values, it is interesting to look at the list of personal characteristics expected from managers in one large multinational firm – Nestlé – as set forth in the company's statement of management and leadership principles:
– courage, strong nerves and composure;
– the ability to learn, an open mind, perceptiveness, "vision";
– the ability to communicate, to motivate and to develop other people;
– the ability to create an innovative climate;
– thinking in context;
– credibility: in other words, "practise what you preach"; a responsible attitude and behaviour;
– understanding of other cultures and of international developments;
– continuous openness to change and ability to manage this change.

Some conclusions

Positive elements predominate. There is an urgent need to communicate the facts and for socially responsible people to encourage others instead of discouraging them with misunderstandings and unfounded doomsday scenarios.

Globalization works with a complex set of drivers; indeed, global companies are as much driven as they are themselves drivers.

All areas will be affected by competition, with the benefits going to the consumer.

To try to slow down the process of globalization would be unfair to all those who never had a chance before to achieve some prosperity. Moreover, it would not work.

Globalization: Some Socio-Cultural Comments

MELBA PADILLA MAGGAY

Historians would tend to attribute much of what is happening globally today to three revolutions which have shaped modern life; the *economic* revolution that started with the mercantile capitalism of the 12th century, the *industrial* revolution of the 18th century, the *political* revolutions which gave rise to the ideologies of the 19th and 20th centuries. Of these three revolutions, the significance of the political one has been sidelined by technology and the market. The nation-state is increasingly rendered borderless by interlocking economic interests and the traffic of information via cyberspace. The market and technology have replaced ideology as a primary force in organizing societies. There is a decided shift towards reliance on market forces in resolving what used to be political questions, and a certain sense of inevitability over the globalization process as technology extends its reach. In this short paper I shall outline the social and cultural impact of this process on many societies today.

The rise of Mammon

With the collapse of socialism, societies have increasingly become market-led. By this is meant not only that countries and their internal policies are being organized around the demands of a globalizing economy, but also that people's lives today are much more determined by economics than previously. The ways in which the market is shaping social organization can be seen in the following global trends:

An homogenized world middle class. One of the promises of globalization is the tremendous redistribution of economic power at the world level. By the end of this decade, it is said, East Asia will have arrived at full economic parity with Europe and North America. A world middle class has emerged, made up mostly of the professional elites of Asia, Latin America and Eastern Europe.

This change in the global balance of power, together with the addition of 2.5 billion people into the world market as previously closed economies have opened up, means that intense competition is now focused on capturing this emergent middle class, whose consumption patterns are now similar to the middle classes of industrial economies. A certain homogenization is taking place, though only at the level of the elite. Consumerism by way of globalization means that societies increasingly experience incongruities: in the Philippines, young urban professionals – "yuppies" – run around with pagers and cell phones in a country where half the population does not have access to potable water. The uneven spread of growth within societies increases discontent and marginalization, especially among the urban poor who witness the life-styles of the affluent and erupt into frustration and violence.

Marginalization of the producers of real goods. Because of the speed with which capital moves across borders and the power of transnational corporations to outsource labour and other services from anywhere in the world, trade will increasingly be in money and ideas rather than actual goods. It is predicted that over the next decade, financial transactions and trade in product patents will grow two to three times faster than the movement of goods. Already, about US$1.5 trillion is circulating in the global market. Fabulous fortunes are made by those in information industries who control software, the price and value of which bears little relationship to actual costs or the direct labour that went into its production. This means that those with real goods to sell – like bananas or cheap labour – will have a far less significant impact on world trade than those with access to mobile capital and technological innovations.

The Philippine economy is a good example of the kind of vulnerability induced by globalization. Much of its vaunted growth rests on such volatile items as overnight portfolio investments and remittances from overseas migrant labour. Meanwhile, its agricultural lands are being eaten up by golf courses for transient tourists – threatening its own food and environmental security. Its capacity for producing *real* goods is diminishing in the face of pressure to be part of the global loop which trades instead in the goods of *virtual* reality.

Individualization and insecurity of the work force. The emergence of "virtual corporations" – firms with a fairly small core of competencies but linked to a network of organizational alliances and external experts – is giving rise to a highly individualized work force, operating in isolation out of an "electronic cottage". More and more highly-skilled professionals depend on short-term contracts, with no job security and none of the usual benefits. In order to compete in the global economy, large transnationals downsize, de-linking corporate profit from employee welfare and security. This growing sense of insecurity in the work-place means that corporate loyalties – a factor which in the past propelled economies like that of Japan to perform at a very high rate of productivity – have become fragile.

Increased inequality in access to growth. The head-on mega-competition which is part and parcel of globalization leads to winner-take-all situations. Those who come out on top win big, and the losers lose even bigger. The biggest losers are the poor, whose levels of education and skills leave them far behind those who are knowledge- and communication-oriented. Moreover, their plight is now left to market forces, as seen in the massive funds being poured into micro-credit as a way of training the poor to adapt and survive in the market. The demonstrated unsustainability of welfare systems in the North has made emergent economies unwilling to bail out those at the edges of life. Hard-working East Asian countries like Singapore see to it that no one gets "a free lunch". A kind of social Darwinism is setting in, judging those who fail to adapt themselves to the market as unfit and leaving them behind.

The problem of social integration

Globalization is not a unilinear expansion of the old village, with its self-contained economy and face-to-face encounters and relationships, to the world level. The term "global village" is a misnomer. Rather, globalization is the rapid and uneven diffusion of modernizing influences from societies which have the power to project and extend themselves globally, made possible by transnational institutions and communication technologies which create the illusion of a global community.

It is true, of course, that distances have collapsed and we are now connected to each other by cyberspace. Migration and mass access to travel have brought peoples and cultures face to face. But this proximity has had mixed results. Fear of being engulfed by mega-societies has made ethnic minorities defensive and self-enclosed, while the pressure of hosting the world's 23 million refugees and 25 million migrant workers has strained the resources of many countries to the point of an ultra-nationalist backlash. The problem of social integration – how to live together in a world that is increasingly diverse and multi-cultural – will define much of the politics of the future.

The following are some features of the social landscape emerging from the globalization process:

Increased cultural antagonism and social alienation. Increased cross-cultural contact does not necessarily create a better understanding of other cultures. Instead, proximity often leads to the hardening of racial stereotypes. It is one thing to see other people and their cultures on our television screens; it is quite another to have them living next door, where we can smell their cooking – or, worse, perceive them as crowding us out of our jobs and living space. Without sufficient understanding of each other's cultural assumptions, cross-cultural encounters cause discomfort and become occasions for confirming preconceptions. As the communication theorist Daniel Katz observed long ago, "the physical barriers to communication are rapidly disappearing, but the psychological obstacles remain".

The contemporary resurgence of fascist parties and ultra-conservative nationalists seeking a return to racial purity or some such imagined cultural past is no accident. The psychological disruption of rootedness invites both violence from the host culture and profound alienation from the sojourner. Filipinos, who are some of the happiest people in the world according to cross-cultural studies, find themselves getting mad and demented, jumping off high-rise buildings in the alien lands where they work.

A retreat to primal identities. The co-existence of many races and ethnicities within one nation-state is not new. What is new is the collapse of belief in great architectonic systems based on ideologies, like the old Soviet empire, or even the idea of the nation-state. In a world where the grand narratives of ideology and nationhood have fallen apart, people seem to be retreating to more primal identities, usually culturally or religiously defined. This is manifested in the reassertion of ethnicity among minorities in mega-societies, and in such diverse conflicts as the "ethnic cleansing" in Bosnia and the Balkan states, the "tribal" wars between Hutus and Tutsis in Rwanda, and the separatism of Muslims in the southern Philippines and of the Basques in Spain. We also see it in the rising assertion by diverse groups of their rights to political space – such as women and gay people, for example. While there is waning confidence everywhere in big government, big business and even big trade unions, there is at the same time a groundswell of small solidarities, communities bound by gender, ethnicity or a common political discourse, all serving as primary sources of meaning and identity.

The rise of political religions – whether "Islamic fundamentalism" or the "Moral Majority" – is perhaps best understood as a reaction to the aberrations of secular capitalist values and to the failure of the liberal humanist agenda as a whole. The return of the old gods and the quasi-religious conflicts that come in their wake are symptoms of a certain nostalgia over the loss of an integrating centre by cultures which have been fragmented by colonization or dislocated by leapfrogs into modernity. Many of the world's peoples see life as religiously rooted because their cultures are. Only the West, with its liberal humanist project of the past 200 years, has managed to secularize and compartmentalize reality, leaving religion, which once served as source of integration, out in the cold. The two-thirds world, still decolonizing and feeling the throes of a society in transition, is rediscovering the power of their traditional religions as a buttress against the homogenizing and modernizing forces of globalization.

A technologically-mediated secondary environment. The impact of media technologies on social formation has been such that the world in which we live is now largely a mediated environment. In other words, our perceptions and life-styles are shaped by inorganic secondary sources and authorities. The story we most believe about our lives is no longer what C.S. Lewis called our "primal history", but the myths and narratives constructed for us by the media. What we call "public discourse" is the space provided by media to competing institutions and social forces – or that most recent locus of hope for democratizing societies, the emergence of "civil society". The public space which the state and the church used to dominate is now accessible only within the terms and conditions set by media.

There was a time when the church did not have to compete for attention in the public arena. In an oral culture, says Harold Innis, it enjoyed an edge over other institutions of society: it lived by celebration, recital of mass, the singing of hymns and the giving and hearing of sermons. In the age of electronic media the church has to compete with other consciousness industries in capturing attention thresholds which no longer resonate to the "high definition" redundancies of rhetoric but are instead attuned to the subliminal associations of fleeting images.

The global reach of media and its cultural exports mean that large masses of people, especially the young, are experiencing cultural discontinuities. Increasingly, the media are replacing the school and the home as a major instrument of education and socialization. Cut off from tradition, people drift into revivalist groups like the Aum cult in Japan or become aimless and lost like the Filipino children growing up without one or both of their parents – who are away working in Hong Kong or somewhere in the Arabian desert. Societies that have modernized and yet seek to keep traditional values, like Singapore, end up with rebellious young people who chafe at the bit that reins them tightly.

Some imperatives

With the ascendancy of the market, we need more than ever to bear witness to the fact that people do not live by bread alone. We must resist the marginalization of human values which accompanies the apotheosis of the market as final arbiter of how social life is to be disciplined and organized.

The market is not competent to address problems of poverty and equity. We cannot leave the plight of the poor to the operations of blind market forces. In a time of "compassion fatigue" and indifference to those who are shunted aside by the bulldozing forces of globalization, the church has a special responsibility to "open your mouth for the dumb, for the rights of all who are left desolate" (Prov. 31:8).

What is needed in a multi-cultural world is not only a sense of pluralism, but a sensitive engagement with both the secular and religious imagination, affirming the sameness as well as the uniqueness of our faith claims. At the same time, the church needs to stand against forces that tend to erode the integrity of cultures. We are told that at the end of time there will be a great multitude praising God from every tongue and tribe and people and nation (Rev. 7:9-12). Neither ethnicity nor nationality will wither away; diversity, not homogenization, is the planned destiny for the world.

The most pervasive effect of a technologically-mediated world does not occur on the level of concepts or even social consequences, but on the level of perception. There has been a shift in orientation from word to image, from the sequentiality of print to the simultaneity of audio-visual media. People no longer respond to any kind of communication that proceeds in a linear, abstract sequence, hence the shift from exposition to entertainment, cognition to feeling. Protestant churches, which have traditionally been text-bound, need to address the problem of connecting with the non-linear, sensory-laden world of today. There is need to incarnate, in our life and witness, the Word that has also become an Image (Col. 1:15).

SOURCES

Steward M. Hoover, "Mass Media and Religious Pluralism", in Philip Lee, ed., *The Democratization of Communication*, Cardiff, University of Wales Press, 1995.

Globalization: Some Socio-Cultural Comments 117

Harold Innis, "The Oral Tradition and Genre", in *Empire and Communication,* Toronto, Univ. of Toronto Press.

Daniel Katz, "Psychological Barriers to Communication," *Annals of the American Academy of Political and Social Science*, 1947.

Marshall McLuhan, *Understanding Media*, New York, McGraw-Hill, 1964.

Ian Morrison and Greg Schmidt, *Future Tense: The Business Realities of the Next Ten Years*, New York, William Morrow, 1994.

Nicanor Perlas, "The Perils of Globalization", *Congressional Briefing Paper*, Quezon City, Philippines, Center for Alternative Development Initiatives, 1996.

Michael Schluter and David Lee, *The R Factor*, London, Hodder & Stoughton, 1993.

Klaus Schwab and Claude Smadja, "Start Taking the Backlash against Globalization Seriously", *International Herald Tribune.*

The Impact of Globalization on Labour and Workers' Lives

DOMINIQUE PECCOUD

The constitution of the International Labour Organization (ILO), written just after the first world war, warns that international competition, by inhibiting the will of certain member nations to introduce social progress, might be "an obstacle in the way of other nations which desire to improve the conditions of workers in their own countries". This early 20th-century argument for creating the ILO points to a reality that remains a burning issue today. In a global market in which goods and capital circulate ever more freely and rapidly, there is a need for labour standards which are observed by every nation.

Consider for example the basic principle of "equal remuneration for work of equal value", which is recognized in the preamble to the ILO constitution. This sound principle – which is an application of the principle of non-discrimination within the context of a nation – can easily be perverted in the context of globalization to lead to a downward levelling of wages for jobs of equal skill, especially low-skilled jobs. When this principle has been implemented at a national level in which freedom of association for workers and the right of collective bargaining are ensured by local laws, minimum wages, set according to the local economic situation, have often been fixed. At the global level, money and even enterprises are more and more mobile all around the world and subject to no global governance, whereas trade unions still bargain at the national level, since this is the only level at which governance can produce and implement laws. Moreover, it is not easy to define a universal minimum wage; income levels cannot be compared from one country to another, since there is no longer any correspondence between labour costs and currency exchange rates. There is thus a need for increased international labour standards universally implemented in local laws.

But what is the minimum set of labour standards to be implemented everywhere and how is it possible to promote their implementation universally?

A set of core social standards

The question of core standards has been discussed since 1994 by the ILO's Governing Body Working Party on the Social Dimension of the Liberalization of Trade. Out of this has come the acknowledgment that the standards chosen should not attack the comparative advantage which the least developed countries derive from their low wages. The liberalization of trade is supposed to help them to enter the world economy and increase their participation in it through access to its markets, gaining a fair share of them in industries in which low-skilled work is a big part of product prices. So the Working Party decided to eliminate all the instruments developed by the ILO which were strongly related to the economic level of a specific country or an historically marked process of production. A core set of workers' rights was then adopted and recognized:
– elimination of forced and child labour;
– non-discrimination on the basis of race, religion, gender;
– freedom of association and collective bargaining.

These last two "freedom rights" already have a special status within the ILO: any government can be prosecuted before the ILO jurisdictional authority if it fails to maintain those rights, whether or not it has ratified the relevant conventions. The specific status given to these two rights is quite understandable: they constitute the bootstrap of social organization, which begins with the existence of representative structures of workers and employers and the possibility for them to discuss and regulate working activity at a national level. Without freedom of association, individual actions will never bring better working standards, especially for those holding low-skilled jobs in developing countries. Since most of these countries have a high rate of demographic increase, any individual worker who appeared to be socially demanding could be fired and replaced by anyone chosen from millions of jobless people. Even in the developed countries of the OECD, there is a strong inverse correlation between the rate of unionized workers and of unemployed persons.

These core rights of course represent only the very beginnings of the road towards social justice. As the World Trade Organization (WTO) comes closer to its mandate of freedom of trade for the benefit of the poorest, this core set of social rights should be expanded, as has happened in Western countries over the nearly 80 years of the ILO's exis-

120 *Sustainability and Globalization*

tence. But this will happen only if there are some efficient incentives to urge the implementation of those universally recognized basic rights. How is this possible?

A possible implementation of basic social rights

For a long time there has been talk of a "social clause" as a condition for entering the world market and benefiting from the freedom of trade promoted by the WTO. Participation in the free market as promoted by the WTO would have been subject to the condition of respect for minimum social standards. This could have turned into a new kind of protectionism, with a great amount of hypocrisy involved in assessing whether or not these minimum standards were being observed. For these reasons, the social clause has been rejected by the members of the WTO, especially the representatives of less developed and newly industrialized nations. At the first WTO international ministers' conference in Singapore, it was decided completely to separate world trade and social concerns, giving the ILO the mission of dealing with the latter.

In his report for the 85th session of the International Labour Conference, the director-general of the ILO proposed that non-governmental actors be mobilized for the development of charters, codes of practice and labels to guarantee the conditions under which consumer articles are manufactured.

A labelling system, implemented by countries only on a voluntary basis, would avoid the anarchy of competing systems developed by consumers' associations and private corporations. Let us illustrate what such a system might look like and how it could be implemented:

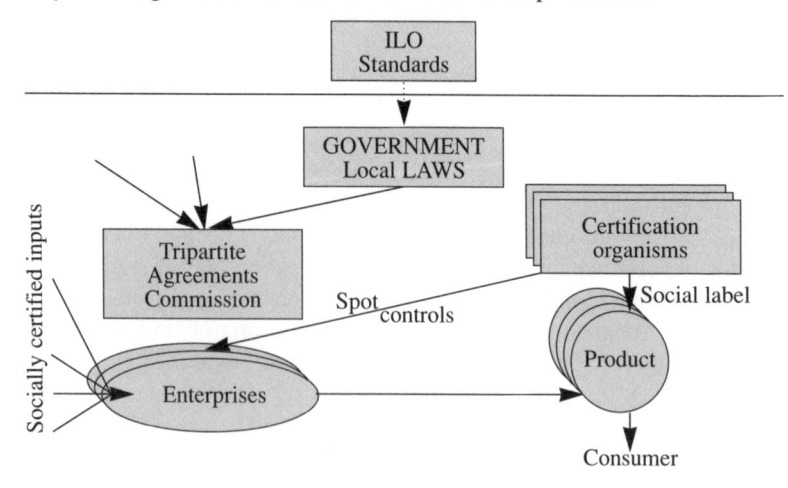

On the basis of the core standards recognized by all the ILO partners, a nation would voluntarily create a tripartite (workers, government, employers) agreements commission, which would define the kind of controls to be applied by certification organisms, following ILO standards adapted to the specific local situation of society. The commission would also make agreements with the independent certification organisms (public or private) which would grant labels to the products of enterprises. The government would be responsible for putting in place and promoting the labellization process. The task of the certification organism would be to study the production process, its social conditions and its inputs. As long as both the inputs into the product and its manufacturing process were certified, the final product itself would be also certified.

Such a process of certification by labelling already functions in the food industry for organically grown products. At one level, this process is similar to the proposed process for "social labelling", since in both cases analysis only of the final product is not always sufficient (to determine, for example, whether it incorporates only organically grown materials or also materials produced using chemical pesticides or fertilizers). Thus it is more a matter of *process control* than of final product control. The big difference is that the controls in the food industry are based on scientifically well-defined criteria (mostly chemical), not on social norms – which are much more difficult to define. In the final analysis, however, labellization is impossible without discriminating criteria to which the response to the question of whether or not they have been applied is yes or no. These criteria must therefore be defined, according to the ILO standards, on a national, tripartite level.

An objection often raised to such a product-oriented social labelling system is that in developing countries it would boost only export-oriented manufacturing and not that which is mainly aimed at local markets. Two answers are possible. The first is that most of the export-oriented manufacturers do a great deal of subcontracting with local structures which also operate for the local market. Since all the inputs of a product must be socially certified, those subcontractors would have to ensure that their practices comply with the social criteria. The second answer is that only products can be labelled, since the information is consumer-oriented. Later, an enterprise-oriented label could be developed for those enterprises all of whose products earn the social label. A further national labelling process would mean that all products coming out of a country merit the social label: this is of course more an horizon than a reachable aim, since even in countries which ratified the conventions associated with the core standards, there would still be enterprises acting against the local laws.

A system of social labelling would have a twofold advantage. First, far from being protectionist, it would foster fair trade by creating a comparative advantage for manufacturers and the nations willing to develop such a process, according to the market demand of the consumers. Second, it would shift responsibility for social cohesion from the level of government to the level of the consumer in everyday life – which is the only way to develop a common sense of social responsibility.

In an initial discussion of the director-general's report – in which this process was proposed in a very general way – the workers' side of the ILO's tripartite structure seemed largely to favour such a labellization process, whereas governments and employers were not so enthusiastic about developing it, particularly in the less developed countries, where as much as 90 percent of the economy is informal even for manufactured goods, through the massive use of uncontrolled home- or sub-contracted work.

This question of a social label raises quite clearly a key issue of globalization. During the 1960s, the developed countries could ignore the poorest ones, and the gap between rich and poor was largely a North-South gap. With the process of globalization, this gap between rich and poor is now widening and is passing through every nation. More than 30 years ago Pope Paul VI warned that "social justice is the new name of peace". More recently, visiting the ILO, James Wolfensohn, the president of the World Bank, expressed a similar view: "a sound social infrastructure is a condition of a sound economic development". How are we to tackle that issue and give it first priority, in order to bridge a gap which seems to be growing wider and wider? Left to its own forces, the market cannot achieve this aim; it is a matter of everyone taking responsibility at his or her own level. Voluntary multilateral measures could be both an expression of and a stimulant for such responsibilities.

Sustainability and Globalization
Demystifying the Single Thought and Single Structure

JOANNES PETROU

Theology has certain aims and functions which remain unchangeable through all ages. But as the world changes, theology must fulfil its task in different space-time and cultural contexts. Thus it has to adapt its analysis to each different reality in order to be faithful to itself and to its mission. The essential task of theology is rightly fulfilled only when it is prophetic. Since exercising this prophetic function means breaking through reality and seeking to develop new relations, theology must have a very good understanding of the reality of its own time.

The function theology has to fulfil is the liberation of men and women and the establishment of their freedom and value. Theology must help human beings to realize the meaning of their life and existence in relation to other human beings. It has to project the basic values and cultivate relations of koinonia, love, peace, solidarity and reconciliation. It has to demystify those powers which grind human beings down and fight against structures which subordinate them to their aims. Moreover, theology must cultivate the principle that human beings are responsible for their neighbours apart from distance, race, gender and colour.

It is evident that all these functions are addressed in a certain context; and it is important to find the specific characteristics of that context and to mark out its dimensions. Over the past decade, Orthodox theology has projected and emphasized the meaning of the person. Theoretically, at least, this emphasis highlights some of the dimensions mentioned above. Yet Orthodox theology has avoided analyzing the structures through which various relations take place (or are prevented from taking place) and the model of society that is formed by or related to these structures. There is thus a risk of individualism, although individualism is something which Orthodox theology does not accept. But anyone who is concerned about the person must also be concerned about the processes and structures which humiliate the person.

This is why it is so important to analyze the structures of society. Only in this way can the human being understand these structures and become aware of his or her freedom and role. It is fundamental first to analyze the environment which subordinates – or in most cases disregards – the person, then to speak about the freedom of the person.

Such an interpretation of the "catholic" in an effort to overcome the existing reality was a common praxis in the ancient Greek and Orthodox tradition. Socrates approached this "catholicity" along the way of self-knowledge. He tried to merge the common characteristics of human beings using the principles of nature and equality. When the apostle Paul dealt with the reality of his time, he understood that a transformation of relations would take place as the church extended to all nations. As the world changed and became church itself, the same would happen to human relations; and the result would be the liberation of human beings. Both Christ and the Revelation to John demystified the symbol and structure of unity of the world of that time, namely the emperor, by insisting that everything comes from God and that the emperor is not God. Things become difficult when the emperor himself becomes a Christian. That means that the empire starts to be considered as the locus of the *Christian utopia*. The fathers of the church took a critical stance over against these developments, formulating the principle that the emperor is God's proper *diakonos*, God's servant, only if he provides the proper foundations for the realization of justice through exercising his legislative task.

Today, of course, the situation is much different. Yet although the world is understood horizontally and not hierarchically, this does not prevent the creation of structures of domination which oppress the human being. Still, the way is open for theology to exercise its prophetic function, provided that it can analyze and understand its contemporary context.

In recent times it has become common to emphasize the significance of the *local context* for theology, especially as a result of the contribution of theologians from the so-called third world. But is it possible to distinguish this local element as something entirely independent of the global context? Orthodox theology has stressed the dimension of locality and the experience of catholicity through the eucharist. But these two elements, locality and catholicity, are developed as though they are to be realized outside of this world and its structures. Such a perception of locality, which does not understand its eschatological dimension deeply enough, fails to bring the hoped-for results precisely because it is not aware of the real dimensions of the place where it performs. Several other unresolved problems arise from this idea that the development of the person's freedom can be fostered without clarifying what theology has to say about society – how it functions, what its dimensions are and when, where and why problems arise. Again it must be emphasized that theology can do its job properly only if it understands the pressures that are being imposed on human beings, only if it grasps the role that social structures play and how it can demystify and humanize those social structures.

The realization is growing that the whole world is actually a village. The world has become universal not only due to the development of communication systems but also because of changing relationships. From international relations and the internationalization of capital-flows, we have moved to *globalization*. The difference between these two dimensions is very important. It is not only a matter of the possibility of free transfer of capital. What is more important is the concentration of power in a very limited number of individuals. This is happening at a worldwide level through the multinational companies which control everything and impose their interests everywhere. The dominant ideology goes beyond borders to impose its own terms and its own choices. Is it possible to develop relationships and structures at the local level independently of this oppressive global framework? Even the question of life and survival is not limited to the local level, but has no limits.

It is necessary to identify some specific characteristics of globalization in order to help us locate the role theology and churches have to play in seeking an antidote – I do not say a solution – to the problems.

Globalization is characterized, first of all, by a certain structure, which of course does not cancel the typical autonomy of local societies, but in fact sets it aside by imposing common directions and options through the homogenization of practice. While these directions and choices have proved to increase problems like poverty, unemployment, social exclusion and other forms of marginalization, globalization includes a mythology of the future whose purpose is precisely to create a feeble acceptance of the problems and a transposition of happiness into the future. It owns institutions, guardians of the dominant interests which replace the role of the state as the guardian of order. The contemporary dominant interests do not have a specific home country.

A certain *single* thought/ideology is being developed, which is the foundation for all choices and activities. Scientific research is oriented to the technocratic utilization of this *single* thought, which acts dogmatically. The acceptance of this *single* thought as the point of reference for all decisions makes compulsion unnecessary. At the same time the dominant means of communication and models of consumption promote the satisfaction of the individual. What is fundamental is the dominance of the economy, its precedence over human beings and nature. The basic norms are of the productive process and productivity, competition and the general idea of the liberal market. The question – to which I shall return – is whether economy is a science or an ideology.

The main question that concerns theology and the churches has to do with the field in which problems are born. During the past decade there was an effort to say that social problems *do* concern the church, that they are also the church's problems and the church must deal with them. (Hidden behind this attitude is an incorrect ecclesiology and an incorrect dichotomy in the understanding of the church-society relationship.) At the same time, the difficulty of dealing with the problems of society has led to another conception: that modern society allows the possibility of developing other ways of life and relationships at its margins. But human beings have a right to live and to define their lives, not a right to marginalization. That is why it is a mistake to face the situation of modern society in this way. It is also a mistake to feel powerless in the face of the domination of the globalized economy and to think that the only alternative is to escape. Problems are growing in society, and we should focus on this point. It is very important for Christians to realize their responsibility as members of society, their responsibility for all that happens around them. Theology must turn itself to this direction and not to any form of escape.

Modern life seems to be divided into spheres. It is claimed that economy has its own unchanging and unchangeable logic. But the main point for human beings is that they live a life which, for all its different facets and confrontations, is unified. Consequently, we should focus our analysis and activity on society. The fact that the modern economy and various contemporary problems are not limited to the local level must not lead to total resignation, but to the achievement of other, broader ways of cooperation. The answer to the globalization of the economy is the creation of a common front against it and the adoption of another holistic thought which will demystify the dominant economic ideology. A weak attitude is never the right approach. But is it possible for someone to react in any other way when he or she is afraid to cancel certain temporary alliances and balances, when he or she cannot escape from the prison of the past and structures that have nothing to do with the present?

This situation results in a transposition of the main interest, which is useful to the dominant system and which it can even finance. This dominant system offers an alibi to its servants. Besides, it is reinforced and it can promote its own theories, such as the well-known theory concerning the "clash of civilizations".

If the main aim of theology is the person and her or his freedom, then its function ought to be analogous. Does theology really mean and believe what it proclaims – or does it just say things? Theology must have a starting point, and this is the human being, each human being, for whom Christ became human. And the human being must constitute the criterion and aim of theology.

If one turns to the relationships of koinonia which theology is supposed to serve, then one must choose either the realities of the globalized economy or the demystification of and organized reaction to it in the service of the human being. And the service *(diakonia)* of the human being means serving his or her liberation.

It seems to me that there is a strange attitude of fear towards economy. Economy ought to be an area of analysis based on the principle that the human being has absolute priority, a basis which leads to the demystification of the powers that grind the person down. Instead, there is fear in the face of the power of the economy. Because we cannot control it, we stand fearful before it. But this is a wrong attitude. Globalization functions as a modern idolatry which we cannot overcome with non-rational exorcisms, but only through analysis and knowledge. Paradoxically, although there is an economic power behind every single modern problem, theological efforts at the analysis of these problems are limited to the level of registering their results or pointing out the role of the intermediate elements (science, technology, biotechnology). Mention of the issue of economy is avoided. The ecological problem is a similar case. Behind it lies the modern economic structure, ideology and practice. Nevertheless, theological efforts to analyze it avoid mentioning the economy itself – as though there were a fear that whatever appeared redeeming would turn out to be the cause of all the problems.

In speaking about the sustainability of the world, one must consider two dimensions: nature and the human being. But the social world cannot be sustainable if it does not care about the consequences for nature and the human being. A society which does not care about its members plants the seeds of its own destruction; and nature suffers from the domination and decline of the contemporary human being. The world cannot survive if it accepts the options imposed by globalization, which returns it to the barbarity of the system in which the powerful impose their will on the weak, in which the workers and those who are weak do not have any achievements and rights, only the powerful.

According to the sociological classification of models of action, economic practice belongs to the realm of rational actions, so characterized because of their aims. The problem is that we do not search for their aim. They appear to be rational and they become autonomous, which means that we are obliged to accept them, since there is no other choice. One of the basic characteristics of the modern world is this "rational" constitution and the "rational" way of production that goes along with it. This conception has created its own objectivities and norms, and it is considered to have created our frame of reference. All these measures are autonomous (independent) from human being and life in general.

In this way economy itself appears as an objective science. But the fact is that it is not a science at all but an ideology, which has no claim to objectivity. Objectivity has to do with a certain basic aim. The study of economy's negative consequences (the different problems that arise) and of its real aim (to serve power) overturns its claim to rationality. Economy should have as its main aim the service of human beings and the preservation of the balance of nature. If we want to assure this, we must work to create a new rationality and a new economic practice – and that is a matter of collective effort.

The priority of economy is a basic principle of the modern world. It is expressed by the dominance of the options for productivity, for the maximization of power and result, for the autonomous and invisible "rules of the game", economic and political. All these expressions of the priority of economy can find no place in a sustainable society, whose priority will be human being, human needs and life. The uncontrolled process of the globalized economic system creates a variety of problems. Serving the aims of economy results in poverty. Economy does not care about homeless people or the destruction of the environment. It produces refugees – and then founds organizations to take care of them. But anyone can see that it would be wiser and more rational to anticipate these sad developments than to deal with their results.

It is impossible to confront any of the situations we have mentioned without a reversal of the priorities of modern society. Otherwise these problems will only increase. This dilemma is easy to understand. Human being and life cannot be the victims of the modern economy. Economy cannot determine human relationships. Humanity must again become the decisive factor, determining its own relationships, defining its own needs, adapting its economic practice to these needs.

All of this affirms that the quality of life and of human relationships must be the criterion for a sustainable society and not the victim of economic pursuits. When we speak about the priority of human being and life, we attack the ways and means of the modern economy. For example, competition is presented as the basic way to regulate economy. But there is abundant evidence that competition is a means of imposition and of redistribution of income, but not of progress. How can anyone speak of solidarity, mutuality and cooperation as the main characteristics of modern progress, when competition is projected as a value?

Many people are coming to realize that it is impossible to leave life to the mercy of the economically powerful and their technocratic decisions and pursuits. On the contrary, the framework of action should be defined by decisions of a political character, based on social consciousness. This requires a certain attitude towards the world and life. Consequently, we need a different way of understanding reality, one that is not based on contradiction and competition and domination, nor on continuous consumption and the production of new needs. It should be based on the limitation of needs, on the discovery of ways to avoid destruction, on the sharing of life with others, on the development of relationships of koinonia among people and on the priority of life over any other expediencies and pursuits. All these positive elements make up a spiritual attitude towards life and relationships, an attitude diametrically opposed to the conception of life based on economic productivity and the individualistic achievement of power and prosperity. This spiritual dimension must be the one which theology and the churches cultivate.

Reclaiming Motherhood
In Search of an Eco-Feminist Vision

ARUNA GNANADASON

My strongest childhood memories are of a guava tree on the farm near Bangalore in India where I grew up. It was a tree particularly conducive to climbing, and my sisters, brothers and I used to spend many an hour sitting on its different branches. One day it was a school classroom, the next a home, on the third day it was a wedding house – to whatever wild extent our imaginations went, the tree accompanied us. As I remember, it gave us fruits at all times of the year – forbidden fruit, since we were not allowed to eat too many, because my mother considered them not very digestible. We spent many joyful hours in that tree.

Trees have always fascinated me. Sometimes they have so gripped my attention that I have found it difficult to write or read if the place where I am offers me a window with a tree opposite it.

No wonder the poet Rabindranath Tagore wrote:

Silence
My soul
These trees are prayers...

Creation, with all the beauty it offers, has always overawed me. Indeed, this has been a strong influence on my theological formation. But I believe that my eco-feminist vision is formed out of another and more mundane reality – the daily struggles of women who are engaged every day "in the production of survival", as the feminist environmentalist Vandana Shiva describes it.[1] Thus this is not some romantic or esoteric vision. It is based on a plea for sanity; it is a cry that we recognize the destruction of the earth as sin. To reverse this destructive madness is an urgent imperative for our times.

The conscious decision to use Larry Rasmussen's term "the earth community" rather than "the environment" points to the conviction of many Asian feminists that the "death of Nature" implies that the survival of the trees, of the air, of the land, of the seas is inextricably linked with the survival and the improvement of the quality of life of all people – particularly women, who bear the greatest consequences of the degradation of the earth.

The expression "integrity of creation" forbids the division of humankind from other kind or of humans from one another. Certainly it challenges the hierarchical dualisms and excessive anthropocentrism that have been at the heart of many traditional Western patriarchal theologies. Unhappily, most liberation theologies (except for eco-centred and feminist liberation theologies) have not provided a strong challenge to these; indeed, the theological methodology of the Ecumenical Association of Third World Theologians has long been aggressively anthropocentric. Only now is there a gradual but slow shift in consciousness. Part of the reason for this is that liberation theologians have basically engaged in dialogue only with the metacosmic religions, which are also patriarchal in content and intent and do not respond to the voices of women, of Dalits, of Indigenous Peoples or of the earth. The discovery of the earth-centred power of the cosmic religiousness of people is a new discovery even for liberation theology.

Eco-feminist theologians have many varied entry points into this discussion. Lois Daly uses the unfortunate expression "competing feminisms" to describe this diversity.[2] I believe we cannot afford to be in competition with each other; instead, we should humbly share our many experiences with each other and learn from each other, offering our plurality of visions to a common concern to affirm life. There are no "competing feminisms", only a wide range of experiential bases which informs our theological visions.

The reality – analysis of oppression

My starting point is women's daily struggle for survival. The attempt is to draw inspiration from the many ways in which women find spiritual resources for their struggle. I speak of Janakibehn, a woman from the Bonda community – one of the indigenous communities in India. She and her people have lived in the Koraput forest district of the state of Orissa for many decades. Suddenly their lives are overturned when the government decides to "develop" them by planting an aluminium production factory in the centre of their lands. The factory literally stamps out the life of the Bonda people, taking away from them not only their land and livelihood, but their culture, their value systems, their very life.

Gabriele Dietrich speaks of women in two other struggling communities in India – a fishing community in Kerala and an urban poor community in Madurai town.[3] She describes the spiritual resources found in their daily struggles for survival, analyzing this from the perspective of their work, their bodies and sexuality, their relationship to the earth, their spirituality, and their struggles to rebuild the structures of their societies. Sex role divisions of work ensure that women do the most strenuous kinds of work *in close proximity to the resources of the earth* – food and fuel gathering and collecting of water from distant places. Women are expected to care for the families, often singlehandedly, while men live wasteful lives. When resources are depleted they must simply travel further in search of food, water, firewood and means of livelihood. But even within the context of their powerlessness over their productive and reproductive capacities, they find the spiritual resources simply to survive.

The exclusion of women from abundant life is deliberate. A 1996 UNICEF report notes that 1 in 13 women in sub-Saharan Africa and 1 in 35 in South Asia die of causes related to pregnancy and childbirth. For Europe the figure is 1 in 3200; for the US 1 in 3300. If this is not deliberate and intentional discrimination against poor women, what is it? The report attributes these frightening figures for South Asia not only to poverty and lack of basic health care facilities but also to inherent "anti-woman" attitudes of South Asian cultures.

Our societies confer a similar low status on the earth. To take the example of India again: we lose 1.3 million hectares of forests each year; soil conditions are deteriorating rapidly, with 56.6 percent of the land suffering water and wind erosion; floods and drought cause serious damage each year; indiscriminate use of water resources (often for heavy industries) is causing a rapid fall in the level of ground water reserves; pollutants, chemical wastes, fertilizers and pesticides are eating into the core of the earth itself.

To understand this, it is necessary to uncover the roots of this crisis which has impoverished millions of people and denied them a life of dignity and in turn places tremendous pressure on the earth. The right to food, which is one of the most basic of human rights that God has provided for the men, women and children of this world, is an elusive dream for millions in our world. Africans would constantly remind us that what they experience is not just marginalization but systematic exclusion. The major reason for this is pervasiveness of the post-colonial model of "development" along the lines of Western science and technology, as a

Reclaiming Motherhood: In Search of an Eco-feminist Vision 133

direct consequence of the industrial revolution in Europe. The entire world has had to model itself on the colonizing West, which itself went through a different history and process of development and did not experience the subjugation and exploitation of being colonized. It was assumed that "Western-style industrial development" was possible for all; and even essentially agricultural countries had to transform their economies to keep pace with industrial expansion.

Such a developmental model "reduces all differences into a flatland called modernity, in which dams displace people and forests and rivers become resources",[4] writes the Indian feminist activist Corinne Kumar. Mountains, forests, rivers and lakes become "resources", considered "productive" only when they can be exploited and "profits" can be extracted from them.

> Against this dominant model of development, technology and nation state power, manipulated by world financial institutions and global market forces, talk of a "new world order" or "North-South dialogue" or "self-reliance" is no more than a political technique for seeking concessions without ever touching the essence of the existing order.[5]

The right to development that governments so often proclaim must be seen together with the silence of governments on the right to livelihood, to health, education and housing.

This concept of "development" is clearly based on capital accumulation and commercialization to generate profits. This implies the creation of not only wealth but also poverty and dispossession. This Euro-centric (and later USA- and Japan-centred) model of development legitimized colonialism and imperialism and subsequently the economic choking of nation after nation in the South. All other civilizations, all other cultures, all other historical experiences, including highly developed systems of philosophical and religious thought, were subordinated to the Western paradigm, seen as a "civilizing force" in a supposedly uncivilized world. It has systematically led to the "death of nature".

> Concepts and categories about economic development and natural resource utilization, which had emerged in the specific context of industrialization and capitalist growth in a centre of colonial power, were raised to the level of universal assumptions and applicability in the entirely different context of basic needs satisfaction for the people of the newly independent third world countries. Yet, as Rosa Luxembourg has pointed out, early industrial development in Western Europe necessitated occupation of the colonies by the colonial powers and the destruction of the "local" (natural) economy.[6]

Now we live in a world in crisis. Everywhere we see the escalation of violence, wars and conflicts. Racial hatred and ethnic tensions are on the increase. Poverty is growing, not only in the familiar places but also in the so-called developed world in the midst of affluence.

We are on the road to the globalization of the market and liberalizing economies. To some sectors of society, this does offer some hope. In India, for example, due to new economic policies approximately 300 million people live consumerist life-styles that compare with those of a middle-class person in the West. But more than 300 million live lower middle-class lives of struggle, and for about 200 million more there is no chance of survival at all. Yet India has been heralded as a success story among the marketizing economies of our world. Alongside the poverty that one cannot ignore is the environmental price India and other countries in the third world are paying. Overcrowded cities accommodate an increase of thousands of cars each day. The pollution is so serious that it is not uncommon to see motorists in large cities wearing masks to cover their nose and mouth. And each day another new car is advertised – from Japan or Korea or Europe. Nor are the rural areas let off the hook. The serenity of the countryside is being destroyed by the denuding of forest lands, the conversion of farmlands for industrial expansion and commercial crops and rapid depletion of water resources which are being channelled into nuclear reactors and other industrial establishments.

Indeed our link with mother earth is completely broken. My concern in this paper is the impact which this development paradigm has had on women like Janakibehn and the land they have revered and worshipped for millions of years. No wonder women have been at the forefront of struggles to challenge the onslaught of violence against them and against creation, for they are the primary victims.

Economic growth as the panacea for all problems is the strategy underpinning the present phase of globalization in our world. The scandal is the concurrent growth of poverty and exclusion of large sections of the population from any share of this economic growth and therefore any semblance of "development" at all. Ironically, despite the globalizing trends there is at the same time a fragmentation of societies and a widening gap between the North and the South in trying to find answers to these difficult questions. Nor has the series of world conferences organized by the UN in the past decade healed this brokenness; if anything, they have deepened the divide between North and South on questions of how to achieve sustainability. The North blames the South for its runaway population growth; the South points the finger at the North for its overconsumption. Reducing the discussion to these opposing trends is neither helpful nor productive.

Search for a new language and a new challenge

We as Christians are also caught in an awkward space between two worlds: a world we trusted and depended on, which we took to be governed by what we considered "universal Christian principles and values", and another world which challenges such a world-view. We now hear new voices of hope from women, from the indigenous peoples of the world, from the excluded and from the earth itself. These strange new voices must be heeded. A major paradigm shift is called for – a journey into the unknown and unfamiliar, a journey into the local, the particular, the specific experiences at the heart of our societies and cultures.

The ecumenical movement is in a privileged position to offer an alternate world-view. Larry Rasmussen's vision of the *ecumenical earth* as the imperative on which we need to dwell, provides a new challenge:

> *Oikoumene* means "the whole inhabited world"... All things belong to an all-inclusive form upon which the life of each depends. Humankind and otherkind are fit together in an undeniable, if precarious and sometimes mean, unity of life and death. We are not so much *at* home *on* earth as we *are* home *as* earth. This is the first truth of earth ecumenics and earth ethics – the integrity of creation. It renders the ecumenical task basic and clear: *to help life not only survive but thrive together indefinitely; that is, it means sustainability.*[7]

Everything is thus centred on the survival and continuation of life – all life, everywhere on earth. Such a world-view would challenge not only the pressures of population growth but also the growing consumerism in all regions. Rasmussen calls for "global citizenship and earth patriotism, with all the attendant duties of 'choosing life' (Deut. 30:19) and living in accordance with the choice".[8]

Such a world-view would convince us of just how interlinked we are globally, exploding familiar myths about the reasons for the degradation of creation. For instance, it would challenge the tendency to use purely demographic yardsticks to evaluate where we are or to blame everything on the consumerism of the North; it would question the limited ways in which we normally define the carrying capacity of the earth. Such a world-view questions globalism of any kind – even an ecologically sensitized global economy. Rasmussen reminds us that "the debt to nature cannot be paid person-by-person in recycled bottles or ecologically sound habits, but 'only in the ancient coin of social justice' (Wolfgang Sachs)".[9]

But perhaps what is most inspiring in this vision of the ecumenical earth is that it affirms equally the values of global stewardship and of local and particular communities living in close harmony with the earth. The global does not substitute for the local; they live in each other. The concept of the ecumenical earth challenges the tendency to universalize all experiences and seek global solutions to all questions – one of the basic reasons we have been unable to find efficient answers to the questions of population growth – and gives space to particular contextual experiences:

> *Oikos* as a vision is not the Enlightenment project of an earth ethic grounded in the universally human as some core that can be stripped of particularity and exist independently of differences generated by race, gender, class and culture. There is no core human nature so solid that differences are normatively insignificant. Nor is the *oikos* an earth ethic held together by universal norms and procedures secured through the power of shared universal reason as a capacity that somehow leaves the peculiar treasures and passions of time and place behind.[10]

In a context of globalization can the ecumenical movement not provide an alternate vision which would stress our global interdependence and then leave it to each community, in its own place, to work out what citizenship in an ecumenical earth requires of us? The earth – and not the limited place in which each one of us lives – will then become the responsibility of all. We will quickly recognize that we can never live in small, exclusive, safe ghettoes, because when one place or when one people suffer all of us suffer. The microcosm and the macrocosm become enmeshed into one.

An Asian feminist theological voice of hope and challenge

Given this vision, I offer the concept of motherhood as a possible theological methodology to redefine our inextricable bond with creation and with each other so that we can walk together into an "ecumenical earth". This is only an exploratory, heuristic model and is certainly not intended to be a romanticization of a concept. Before exploring this, let me make three introductory remarks:

1. I do not see "motherhood" as a purely biological role but as a social and theological construct opening up a radical new way to understand our relationship to the world, ourselves and one another. I am aware of the idealization of motherhood to domesticate women in many cultures – and in the church. What I am trying to do is to reclaim moth-

erhood from patriarchal control and to announce it as a model for our times. However, it is significant that mother goddesses are most often represented as virgin, mother and fertility symbol; therefore, they represent creativity, regeneration and sustainability. This therefore affirms their sexuality, their power to re-create and regenerate life. In other words they are strong symbols of sustainability.

2. I am not reducing the discussion to the discovery of the motherhood of God, although this issue continues to be important, because we have lost the power of the feminine in much of our spirituality. I believe we have been forced to seek feminine images of God because patriarchy has taken away from us the Mother of God. But by simply substituting a feminine image of God for a masculine image of God we are not touching the spiritual roots of the problem – that religion has lost some of its power to offer a word of hope, comfort and caring.

3. Explorations into the concept of motherhood go hand in hand with struggles for political, economic, social and religio-cultural reconstruction of our societies. The search for a new relationship with creation is as much economic, political and ideological as it is theological. The theological reconstruction is intended to offer a word of hope to both women and men in our daily struggles for justice, peace and the integrity of creation.

Let me begin by drawing on Indian spirituality to show the power of feminine energy as an integral part of the culture and society. Much of my eco-feminist thought has been deeply inspired by Indian spirituality.

In pre-Aryan thought in India, nature was symbolized as the embodiment of the dynamic feminine principle *shakti* (energy, power), the source and substance of everything. *Prakriti* (nature) manifests this primordial energy. Throughout the centuries women have drawn their *shakti* from *prakriti*. Concepts such as *bhudevi* (goddess earth) and *bhumatha* (mother earth), which are used in the people's everyday parlance, emphasize this.

Itwari Devi, a woman leader in the struggle against mining operations in the Utharkhand region of the Himalayas in India, describes how women have drawn energy from nature to sustain their struggles:

> Our power is nature's power, our *shakti* (power) comes from *prakriti* (nature). Our power against the contractor comes from these inner sources, and is strengthened by his trying to oppress and bully us with his false power of money and muscle. We have offered ourselves, even at the cost of our lives, for a peaceful protest to close this mine, to challenge and oppose the power that the government represents. Each attempt to violate us had strengthened

our integrity. They stoned our children and hit them with iron rods, but they could not destroy our *shakti*.[11]

The image of the links between women and creation should not be stretched too far. But these simple women demonstrate, in their own words, that it is women who have been most concerned to maintain the bond with creation, for they have a vested interest in conserving the resources of the earth, the essentials for their everyday survival. The violence of "development" and the violence inflicted on creation are linked closely with violence against women. Both women and creation are to be appropriated, used, abused and discarded when considered "worthless". Both land and woman may be *virgin*, untouched by man. They may both be *raped*. They are both prized if *fertile*, despised or rejected if *barren* – and the reproductive capacity of both are artificially manipulated to make them fertile.

In all civilization the care and nurture of the earth have been closely linked with the image of the mother goddess. Often synonymous with mother earth, she has been a strong symbol of fertility, agriculture and life. The use of vegetation – flowers and leaves – in worship is symbolic of this. The image of the mother goddess, wherever found, inspires and focuses the perception of the universe as an organic whole. For example, archaeologists have unearthed terracotta images of the mother goddess at every stage of Indian history, dating back to the 6th millennium B.C.E.:

> Fired or left unbaked, depending on the rituals for which they were intended, these icons of the mothers, the holders of the secrets of the earth, epitomized magical rites of agriculture, fertility, life and death. At the time of sowing of seeds and harvesting and in rituals to dead ancestors, icons of the virgin mothers were made of clay, installed, worshipped and then cast into the waters, or offered to ancient sites of the goddess – to caves, clearings, in forests or to the trees – or abandoned at village boundaries. By their very nature impermanent, the earth mothers could not be kept under the householder's roof, except for short ritual purposes.[12]

She was of the earth and into the earth she would blend to replenish it and give it creativity, fertility and power.

The imperative of reclaiming this symbol

Our link with mother earth is broken. Today we measure her value only in terms of the profit we can draw from her. Through a patriarchalization of our societies and our spiritual heritage, we have lost the power of the mother goddess, who could have been our source of hope. We need to reclaim her power and this is what Asian women are attempting to do.

Motherhood plays a crucial role in Asian feminist methodology because the creative principle is at the heart of the feminist consciousness. Denying themselves a life of their own, women have been engaged in creating and sustaining life for all. In Indian society a woman's selfhood generally depends on the life of the community. The creative, nurturing urge, rooted in giving birth to and protecting new life, is surrounded with ceremony and rituals in many Indian homes, affirming of the fertility associated with the earth and the gifts nature bestows on us.

Yet feminist hermeneutics cannot ignore the fact that this creative and self-sacrificing love of women is idealized and abused to restrict women's time, space and movement. Therefore, a new definition of the creativity of motherhood and of the "feminine" – as a source of new life wherever there is death – is needed. The creative power of Indian women in movements against deforestation and mining operations is reminiscent of the mothering feminist power of the two midwives Shiprah and Puah in the Exodus story (Ex. 1:15f.). These women protected life through the only form of resistance open to them. The sexuality, fertility and creative power of women must be reclaimed from the distortions and control of patriarchy.

In Indian culture, blood is a powerful symbol of fertility. Kali's rampage, in her quest to destroy evil, could be appeased only by blood sacrifices. The Khamakya temple in Guwahati, Assam, is dedicated to the female genitals *(yoni)*. There is no image of the goddess in this temple but in a cave in the depths of the shrine is a *yoni*-shaped cleft in the rock which is kept moist with a blood-like flow caused by a natural spring. After the first monsoon rains, a great ceremony is performed when the water, mixed with the iron-oxide in the rocks, runs red, symbolizing menstrual blood. The Melmaravathoor temple near Madras is dedicated to the goddess Adi Parasakti (the supreme form of female power), another fertility mother goddess. Here, women in red sarees (and, in recent years, men in red dhothis) worship the gift of fertility, creativity and life.

Many other examples of the worship of the cosmic womb and the blood that flows from it, symbolizing the creative principle, could be cited. Despite the onslaught of patriarchal forces, these life-giving, women-centred fertility cults have endured in India. It is important to reclaim these powerful symbols of the creativity of women, drawing inspiration from blood – that which cleanses and purifies, preparing the environment for new life. "This is my blood of the new covenant, which is shed for many..." (Matt. 26:28).

Of course, it is not only in India's pre-patriarchal religious history that these powerful symbols are found. There is Isis from ancient Egypt, Pachamama the earth mother of the indigenous peoples of the Americas, Cybille the ancient Greek mother goddess. The mother goddess Artemis of Ephesus acquired her form as an extremely fertile woman in 7000 B.C.E. She was the mother of all, the most powerful being who ruled everything. Her influence spread to the four corners of Anatolia, then to Mesopotamia, Egypt, Arabia and even Scandinavia. What interests me most about this beautiful goddess is that she was worshipped as goddess of fertility. Her robes are made of animals, because she was seen as protectress of animals. This many-breasted goddess was a symbol of the productive forces of nature, of creativity, fertility, regeneration and therefore sustainability.

There have been constant efforts to stamp out or suppress the feminine principle and the mother goddess. But as we see in the history of India and elsewhere in the world, she remains in the hearts and faith of many people in their popular religiousness.

What of Christianity?

I have begun a new search, still tentative but I believe important. Let me begin by quoting Anne Baring and Jules Cashford:

> In Judeo-Christian mythology there is now, formally, no feminine dimension of the divine, since our particular culture is structured in the image of a masculine God who is beyond creation, ordering it from without; he is not within creation as were the mother goddesses before him. This results, inevitably, in an imbalance of the masculine and the feminine, which has fundamental implications for how we create our world and live in it.[13]

True as this statement is, I am no longer satisfied with it. For too long I had based my eco-feminist explorations on ancient Indian spirituality. I still feel that this can be a source of inspiration, but it is also a challenge to look with new eyes at the Christian heritage. What can we reclaim and discover anew in our faith heritage to offer us a word of hope? Cashford and Baring continue:

> Even when the goddess myth was debased and devalued *it did not go away, but continued to exist in disguise – from images that were prevented from expressing themselves vitally and spontaneously, particularly in the Judeo-*

Christian tradition... The myth of the goddess continued to act on the prevailing world-view of the time. However, since this myth was contrary to formal doctrine, its action had to be implicit and indirect in the manner of any less-than-fully conscious attitude, which meant that its unacknowledged but persistent presence often distorted even the finest expressions of the prevailing myth of the God. It seemed clear that the feminine principle was an aspect of human consciousness that could not be eradicated.[14]

I would contend that in Mary the Mother of Jesus we have a source of hope. Mary has been given many titles in Christian history – Guarantee of the Incarnation, Virgin Mother, Second Eve, Mother of God (Theotokos), Immaculate and Assumed into Heaven. The precise nature of Mary's participation as Co-redemptrix with Christ is still a controversy. Of all these titles, what is particularly important is her recognition by the council of Ephesus in 431 as Mother of God, the Theotokos. Like the mother goddesses who went before her she was both virgin and mother. She too could have been a strong symbol of fertility and regeneration and therefore of sustainability, but this was suppressed. One explanation offered for this is the growth in early Christian history of an ascetic movement which resisted the immoral life-styles, pomp and political machinations of the leadership of the church. This helped to encourage the model of Mary as perpetual virgin, depriving her of her sexuality and therefore her fertility. Such a theory found support in the Song of Solomon: "A garden locked is my sister, my bride, a garden locked, a fountain sealed" (4:12). Such an image affirms her virginity but also her sexuality. Note also in this text the presence of vegetation – so much in keeping with the mother goddesses of old.

The church venerated Mary and lifted her beyond human reach by making her pure, beyond all sin, the highest of all creatures. Finally in 1950, Pope Pius XII made the dogma official: "The Immaculate Mother of God, the ever Virgin Mary, when the course of her earthly life was run, was assumed in body and soul to heavenly glory." But, in popular religiousness, devotion to Mary as Mother has remained strong through the centuries, particularly in the daily spirituality for struggle and survival of women.

Veneration of the Mother of God received impetus when the Christian church came under the imperial church under Constantine and the "pagan" masses came under Christian influence and became members of the church. The people of the Mediterranean and the Middle East could not make themselves conversant with the absolute power of God the Father and the strict patriarchalism of the Jewish idea of God, which the original Christian message had taken over. Their piety and religious consciousness had been formed for millennia through the cult of the Great Mother Goddess and the Divine Virgin, a development that led all the way from the popular religions of Babylonia and Assyria to the mystery cults of the late Hellenistic period... In Egypt, Mary was, at an early point, already worshipped under the title Theotokos.[15]

It is the patriarchalization of the divine that has compelled feminist theologians to search the Christian scriptures and the faith of people to find a feminine image of God. In Indian spirituality, this was not necessary because of the prominence of the mother goddesses in the divine pantheon. The most powerful symbol of the presence of both the female and male elements is the image of *Ardhanariswara*, the male-female figure of Shiva and Parvathi – symbolizing the inseparable links between the male and female. But God also appears in animal forms, the elephant-headed Ganapathi who protects us from all dangers, the monkey God Hanuman who symbolizes loyalty and love. In the minds and hearts of worshippers, God is divine, beyond all earthly constructions. Do we as Christians need a feminine image of God when we have the Mother of God? God as mystery is beyond our human understanding, but the Mother of God can be brought closer to us, to our need for searching divine inspiration to pray for and work for a healing of the earth, for regeneration, creativity and sustainability.

A feminist eco-vision offers many sources of meaning and hope. It provides a desperately needed alternative vision. It is not an attempt to find universal theological principles for all times; it is simply an offering at the table, a contribution from which we can develop a new ethic, a new understanding of the earth, of our place on the earth and of our relationship to the earth, to each other and to God.

NOTES

[1] Vandana Shiva, *Staying Alive: Women, Ecology and Development*, London, Zed Books, 1989.
[2] Lois K. Daly, "Ecofeminism, Reverence for Life and Feminist Theological Ethics", in Charles Birch, William Eakin and Jay B. McDaniel, eds, *Liberating Life: Contemporary Approaches to Ecological Theology*, Maryknoll NY, Orbis, 1990, p.93.
[3] Gabriele Dietrich, "The World as Body of God", in Rosemary Ruether, ed., *Women Healing Earth: Third World Women on Ecology, Feminism and Religion*, Maryknoll NY, Orbis, 1996, pp.82ff.
[4] Corinne Kumar, "The Universality of Human Rights Discourse", in Aruna Gnanadason, Musimbi Kanyoro and Lucia Ann McSpadden, eds, *Women, Violence and Non-Violent Change*, Geneva, WCC, 1996, p.32.
[5] *Ibid.*, p.32.
[6] Vananda Shiva, *op. cit.*, p.1.
[7] Larry Rasmussen, *Earth Community, Earth Ethics*, Geneva, WCC Publications, 1996, p.90 (emphasis added).

8 *Ibid.*, p.93.
9 *Ibid.*, p.142.
10 *Ibid.*, p.94.
11 Vananda Shiva, *op. cit.*, pp.208-209.
12 Arthur Avalon, *Hymns to the Goddess*, p.118, quoted by Pupul Jayakar in *The Earth Mother*, Harmondsworth, UK, Penguin, 1989, pp.49-50.
13 Anne Baring and Jules Cashford, *The Myth of the Goddess: Evolution of an Image*, London, Penguin, 1993, p.xi.
14 *Ibid.*, p.xii.
15 *Encyclopedia Britannica*, Micropedia, vol. 7, p.279.

About the Contributors

Edward Dommen is professor of economics at the University of Sunderland, England, and a consultant to the WCC's Unit III: Justice, Peace and Creation.

Daniel Rush Finn is professor of economics at St John's University, Collegeville, Minnesota, USA.

Petra von Gemunden is professor of New Testament at the Protestant Faculty of Theology of the University of Geneva, Switzerland.

Aruna Gnanadason is responsible for the Women's Desk of the WCC's Unit III: Justice, Peace and Creation.

Jackie Leach Scully is a biochemist and scientific communicator from the UK.

Melba Padilla Maggay is a social scientist at the Institute for Studies in Asian Church and Culture, Quezon City, Philippines.

Herbert Oberhänsli is assistant to the chairman of Nestlé in Vevey, Switzerland.

Janos Pasztor, a physicist, is coordinator of the Conference and Information Support Programme of the Secretariat of the UN Framework Convention on Climate Change in Bonn, Germany.

Dominique Peccoud is adviser for socio-religious affairs at the International Labour Office, Geneva, Switzerland.

Joannes Petrou is professor of social ethics at the University of Saloniki, Greece.

Peter Tulloch is a trade economist and a member of the Church of Scotland.

Lukas Vischer, formerly director of the WCC's secretariat on Faith and Order, is professor of theology at the University of Bern, Switzerland.

Francis Wilson is professor of economics at the University of Cape Town, South Africa.